BABY SMARTS

Games for

Dedication

This book is dedicated to all of the amazing babies throughout the world.

Acknowledgments

Many thanks to

☆ Anne Meeker Miller, who contributed the signing games in this book

☆ My wonderful editor, Kathy Charner, whom I have worked with for many years

☆ Larry Rood and Leah Curry-Rood, who have supported my work and given me much encouragement

Other books by Jackie Silberg:

125 Brain Games for Babies: Simple Games to Promote Early Brain Development

125 Brain Games for Toddlers and Twos: Simple Games to Promote Early Brain Development

Brain Games for Babies, Toddlers, and Twos: 140 Fun Ways to Boost Development

Games to Play with Babies, Third Edition

Games to Play with Toddlers, Revised

Games to Play with Two-Year-Olds, Revised

Go Anywhere Games for Babies

Baby Smarts

GAMES FOR PLAYING AND LEARNING

Jackie Silberg

Illustrated by Deborah Johnson

gryphon house®, inc.

Beltsville, Maryland, USA

© 2009 Jackie Silberg
Published by Gryphon House, Inc.
PO Box 207, Beltsville, MD 20704
800.638.0928; 301.595.9500; 301.595.0051 (fax)

Visit us on the web at www.gryphonhouse.com

You can arrange to have Jackie Silberg speak, present, train, or entertain by
contacting her through Gryphon House, PO Box 207, Beltsville, MD 20704-0207,
800.638.0928, or at jsilberg@interserv.com.

Illustrations: Deborah Johnson. Cover Art: stockxpert.com.

Library of Congress Cataloging-in-Publication Information
Silberg, Jackie, DATE
  Baby smarts : games for playing and learning / by Jackie Silberg.
    p. cm.
  ISBN 978-0-87659-065-2
  1. Games. 2. Infants--Recreation. 3. Infants--Development. 4. Parent and child. I.
Title.
  GV1203.S535 2009
  790.1'922--dc22
                         2008030358

Bulk purchase
Gryphon House books are available for special premiums and sales promotions as
well as for fund-raising use. Special editions or book excerpts also can be created to
specification. For details, contact the Director of Marketing at Gryphon House.

Disclaimer
Gryphon House, Inc. and the author cannot be held responsible for damage,
mishap, or injury incurred during the use of or because of activities in this book.
Appropriate and reasonable caution and adult supervision of children involved in
activities and corresponding to the age and capability of each child involved is
recommended at all times. Do not leave children unattended at any time. Observe
safety and caution at all times.

Green Press Initiative
Gryphon House is a member of the Green Press Initiative, a
nonprofit program dedicated to supporting publishers in their
efforts to reduce their use of fiber-sourced forests. This book is
printed on paper using 30% post-consumer waste. For further information, visit
www.greenpressinitiative.org.

TABLE OF CONTENTS

INTRODUCTION

Babies are amazingly smart! The more I spend time with them, the more I realize how much they know and understand.

As we find out more and more about the brain, we are learning something that we knew all along—that if babies form loving attachments to adults and have the opportunity and encouragement to explore and experience their environment, they will be prepared for learning throughout their lives.

In the first years of life, the brain is busy building its wiring system. Activity in the brain creates tiny electrical connections called synapses. The amount of stimulation babies receive has a direct effect on how many synapses are formed. Repetitive stimulation strengthens these connections and makes them permanent; connections that don't get used eventually die out.

Smart babies don't need expensive toys. Roll a ball to a baby to develop his muscle coordination. Sing songs and talk to your baby to develop her language abilities. Create patterns with cereal boxes or blocks to develop his math skills.

Facts that researchers from the United States Department of Health and Human Services and elsewhere have discovered include the following:
☆ Babies have a biological need and desire to learn.
☆ The networking of the brain's synapses is nearly complete after the first three years of life.
☆ The more stimulating experiences you can give your baby, the more circuitry the brain builds for enhanced learning in the future.

- ☆ Babies have a preference for high-contrast images.
- ☆ The number of connections in the brain can increase or decrease by 25% depending on how stimulating the environment is.
- ☆ Visual stimulation may enhance your baby's curiosity, attentiveness, and concentration.
- ☆ Your baby's best toy is you! Interact with your baby as much as possible.

The chapters in this book are divided into the following 3-month periods: birth to 3 months, 3–6 months, 6–9 months, and 9–12 months. Each chapter outlines the typical developmental milestones for that age and the games and experiences that develop the skills to reach those milestones.

If you already play some of these games, this book will remind you why they are important. In addition, you will find new ideas for games that you know and ideas for new games and experiences.

Keep the following in mind as you play with your baby:

- ☆ Your baby will like certain games more than others. Play the favorites over and over. Repetition produces growth and development.
- ☆ Stimulate your baby with love and affection by kissing, hugging, gently touching, and speaking lovingly to her.
- ☆ Talk to your baby with expression in your voice. Use words to describe what your baby might see or experience.
- ☆ Respond to your baby's cries as quickly as possible. This makes him feel secure and safe.
- ☆ Make it easy for your baby to imitate your facial expressions and the sound of your voice.
- ☆ Go for walks, travel to different surroundings, and experience different places with your baby. A few examples are: strolling up and down your street to familiarize your baby with the

surroundings; visiting local landmarks such as parks, grocery stores, and libraries; and watching people swim, skate, or run.

☆ Help your baby explore different textures and temperatures.

☆ Read books to your baby. She will love looking at the pictures and hearing the sound of your voice.

☆ Play music and sing. Music stimulates the neurons in the brain that are used for math and logic.

☆ Appreciate, love, and respect your baby. Remember that he is amazingly smart!

Notes from the Author About Interacting with Babies

Playing with a baby is a delightful experience. Babies smile, they giggle and coo, their eyes are wide open with interest. However, too much stimulation can overload a baby's neural circuits, leaving her crying or unsettled. This is your baby's way of saying, "I've had enough."

Signs that playtime or interactions are overwhelming your baby include when your baby closes his eyes, turns away, tenses up and arches his back, avoids your gaze, or begins to get irritable.

When feeding your baby, loud background sounds can be distressing and distracting, and may cause your baby to have indigestion. When babies are finished eating, they need gentle movements until their bodies have digested the food.

At bedtime or naptime, singing lullabies, talking softly, and stroking your baby's back may help her fall asleep. Avoid any over-stimulating experiences, such as loud noises and boisterous actions.

DEVELOPMENTAL CHARTS

Babies from Birth to 3 Months Old

Physical Development

Babies who are up to 3 months old may

- ☆ Hold a rattle
- ☆ Lift their head and chest when lying on their stomach
- ☆ Follow moving objects with their eyes
- ☆ Stretch their limbs all the way out
- ☆ Want visual stimulation
- ☆ See things about 10 inches away

Social-Emotional Development

Babies who are up to 3 months old may

- ☆ Begin to respond to familiar voices
- ☆ Stare at objects or faces of people
- ☆ React to and be comforted by many kinds of sounds
- ☆ Smile at faces
- ☆ Like when people or objects touch their skin

Intellectual Development

Babies who are up to 3 months old may

- ☆ Discover their hands and feet
- ☆ Enjoy feeling different textures
- ☆ Recognize familiar faces and scents
- ☆ Be aware of their left and right sides
- ☆ Begin to connect sounds with their sources
- ☆ Distinguish different voices, qualities, and tone

Babies from 3–6 Months Old

Physical Development

Babies who are 3–6 months old may

☆ Wiggle forward on the floor
☆ Roll over in both directions
☆ Grab an object that is near their hands
☆ Grasp a toy
☆ Hold their head up for a long time without bobbing
☆ Play with their hands and feet
☆ Be aware of many sounds
☆ Be aware of their arms and legs

Social-Emotional Development

Babies who are 3–6 months old may

☆ Babble ("ba-ba")
☆ Gurgle, coo, and squeal
☆ Respond to verbal cues
☆ Watch as you move your mouth
☆ Study faces
☆ Respond to experiences that stimulate their senses
☆ Like to play
☆ Smile responsively
☆ Like social interaction

Intellectual Development

Babies who are 3–6 months old may

☆ Be aware that people and things have labels ("Dada")
☆ Be developing memory
☆ Be aware of their environment
☆ Begin to understand taking turns

Babies from 6–9 Months Old

Physical Development

Babies who are 6–9 months old may

- ☆ Bang objects together
- ☆ Get up on all fours and rock
- ☆ Lunge forward or start crawling
- ☆ Reach accurately for objects
- ☆ Drag objects toward themselves
- ☆ Sit with little support

Social-Emotional Development

Babies who are 6–9 months old may

- ☆ Like to be cuddled and held
- ☆ Jabber and combine syllables
- ☆ Point at objects
- ☆ Want to touch everything
- ☆ Produce a variety of sounds
- ☆ Enjoy nursery rhymes
- ☆ Make two-syllable held sounds
- ☆ Like to look at their reflections in a mirror
- ☆ Enjoy dropping things on purpose
- ☆ Enjoy hearing different volumes and pitches of sounds
- ☆ Enjoy fast and slow rhythms
- ☆ Become aware of body sounds

Intellectual Development

Babies who are 6–9 months old may

- ☆ Learn the names of body parts
- ☆ Study objects
- ☆ Analyze what to do with a toy
- ☆ Understand object permanence

Babies from 9–12 Months Old

Physical Development

Babies who are 9–12 months old may

- ☆ Master crawling with their tummy off the ground
- ☆ Wiggle, kick, and shake their legs
- ☆ Enjoy putting objects into containers
- ☆ Pick things up using a pincer grasp
- ☆ Have good hand and finger coordination
- ☆ Transfer objects from one hand to the other, and then back
- ☆ Enjoy feeling different textures
- ☆ Like to roll balls
- ☆ Clap their hands or wave bye-bye, if prompted
- ☆ Walk with help

Social-Emotional Development

Babies who are 9–12 months old may

- ☆ Say "no" and shake their head
- ☆ Like to look at books with you
- ☆ Copy and imitate your actions
- ☆ Like to sing
- ☆ Laugh at funny things
- ☆ Say several words

Intellectual Development

Babies who are 9–12 months old may

- ☆ Say "Mama" and "Dada" to the correct person
- ☆ Understand the meaning of words in context
- ☆ Follow simple directions
- ☆ Recognize pictures in books or magazines
- ☆ Begin to understand cause and effect
- ☆ Understand the meaning of words they hear
- ☆ Like to pretend
- ☆ Understand the signs that they have learned
- ☆ Respond to familiar questions with actions or words

1

FOR BABIES FROM BIRTH TO 3 MONTHS OLD

Physical Development

Babies who are up to 3 months old may

☆ Hold a rattle
☆ Lift their head and chest when lying on their stomach
☆ Follow moving objects with their eyes
☆ Stretch their limbs all the way out
☆ Want visual stimulation
☆ See things about 10 inches away

Social-Emotional Development

Babies who are up to 3 months old may

☆ Begin to respond to familiar voices
☆ Stare at objects or faces of people
☆ React to and be comforted by many kinds of sounds
☆ Smile at faces
☆ Like when people or objects touch their skin

Intellectual Development

Babies who are up to 3 months old may

☆ Discover their hands and feet
☆ Enjoy feeling different textures
☆ Recognize familiar faces and scents
☆ Be aware of their left and right sides
☆ Begin to connect sounds with their sources
☆ Distinguish different voices, qualities, and tone

Games and Experiences to Develop Babies' Physical Skills

Gentle Sounds

Developmental milestone: Babies who are up to 3 months old may hold a rattle.

- ☆ Find toys that make gentle sounds when you move them.
- ☆ Move close to your baby and shake or move the toy so it makes a soft sound.
- ☆ The sound will draw your baby's attention to the toy and he may reach out his hands to hold the object.
- ☆ If you place the toy in his hand he may grasp it.

On the Ball

Developmental milestone: Babies who are up to 3 months old may lift their head and chest when lying on their stomach.

- ☆ Sit in front of a large inflatable ball.
- ☆ Hold your baby securely as you place him on the ball, facing you with his tummy on the ball so he can lift his head and chest.
- ☆ While you continue to hold him securely, gently roll the ball back and forth a short distance.
- ☆ Add to this experience by making funny sounds.
- ☆ The motion of the ball is relaxing for your baby and he will enjoy watching your face as you make funny sounds.

Fly Away

Developmental milestone: Babies who are up to 3 months old may lift their head and chest when lying on their stomach.

- ☆ Flying games stimulate the parts of the brain that maintain a sense of balance.
- ☆ If your baby can hold his head up without support, his neck muscles are strong enough for flying games, which babies enjoy very much.
- ☆ Use gentle, controlled lifts to protect your baby's back and head.
- ☆ Say, "Fly, fly, little bird, now it's time to land." As you say "fly, fly," hold your baby high in the air, and when you say "land," bring him down to your chest.

Shake the Rattle

Developmental milestone: Babies who are up to 3 months old may follow moving objects with their eyes.

- ☆ Slowly move a rattle from left to right so your baby can follow the rattle with his eyes.
- ☆ Notice if your baby stops following the rattle when you get to the center.
- ☆ If your baby stops watching the rattle, shake it gently until he is focused on the rattle again, then continue to move the rattle to the right.
- ☆ When your baby uses his eyes to focus on something that crosses the midpoint of the body, this helps wire his brain effectively, connecting the right and left hemispheres.

Chop, Chop

Developmental milestone: Babies who are up to 3 months old may follow moving objects with their eyes.

✮ Play this game with your baby by slowly moving your fingers in front of his eyes.

✮ Say, "Chickie, chickie, chop, chop" as you open and close your fingers and move them from one side to the other.

✮ Say the words three times and then give your baby a gentle kiss.

A Beam of Light

Developmental milestone: Babies who are up to 3 months old may follow moving objects with their eyes.

✮ When the room is dark, shine a beam of light from a flashlight on an object in the room.

✮ Sing your baby's favorite song as you slowly move the beam of light to the rhythm of the song.

✮ This game develops your baby's ability to track moving objects.

Moving Fingers

Developmental milestone: Babies who are up to 3 months old may follow moving objects with their eyes.

✮ When your baby is alert and relaxed, place him on his back.

✮ Bring your right hand in front of his eyes and slowly bend your index finger up and down, followed by the middle finger, then the fourth finger, and then the little finger.

☆ When he notices your fingers, move them slowly from left to right. He should be following your fingers with his eyes.

☆ This game develops your baby's tracking skills.

Up and Down

Developmental milestone: Babies who are up to 3 months old may follow moving objects with their eyes.

☆ When you notice that your baby is focused on a toy, slowly move it up and down and back and forth to develop his tracking skills. This also develops the neck muscles.

☆ As you move the toy around, say, "Watch the toy, up and down. Watch the toy, 'round and 'round. Up and down, 'round and 'round. Watch the toy, stop!"

☆ When you say "stop," hold the toy still.

Exercise!

Developmental milestone: Babies who are up to 3 months old may stretch their limbs all the way out.

☆ Exercise your baby's leg muscles.

☆ Place your baby on his back on a comfortable surface.

☆ Cup his feet in the palms of your hands and gently move his legs up and down, and then side to side in a circular motion.

Go Outside

Developmental milestone: Babies who are up to 3 months old may want visual stimulation.

☆ A great way to offer your baby some visual stimulation is to take your baby outside.

☆ Sit with him as he enjoys watching the wind blow the leaves on a tree, watching the interplay of light and shadow, or seeing birds and airplanes in the sky.

☆ Talk to him about what he may be noticing.

I See You!

Developmental milestone: Babies who are up to 3 months old may want visual stimulation.

☆ Place your baby in new places and new positions so he can see you from different angles.

☆ Place your baby where he can see you and say, "Hello, sweet baby. I love you."

☆ As you say the words, do different things with your body. Sit down on the floor, put your head between your legs with your back to your baby, or move your arms in different ways.

☆ Your baby will need to search his surrounding to find the source of your words. This will challenge and stimulate him.

Smile!

Developmental milestone: Babies who are up to 3 months old may want visual stimulation.

☆ Hold your baby with both hands, supporting his back and head.
☆ Keep your hands in a stationary position as you slowly move your head from side to side.
☆ Be sure that you are making eye contact with your baby at all times.
☆ Move your head to one side. As you move to the other side, stop at the midline and smile. Then, move to the other side.
☆ Continue going back and forth with a smile at the midline.
☆ Now try winking at the midline and see if your baby will try to copy you.

I Like This View!

Developmental milestone: Babies who are up to 3 months old may see things about 10 inches away.

☆ Place your baby in new places and new positions so that he can see you and others from different angles.
☆ Some different places could be on the floor, in front of a window, or propped up on pillows.

Games and Experiences to Develop Babies' Social-Emotional Skills

Sing-Song Voice

Developmental milestone: Babies who are up to 3 months old may begin to respond to familiar voices.

☆ Hold your baby and talk to him using a sing-song voice.
☆ Say simple things that you notice about your baby or about the surroundings. "Here are your ears." "I see your nose." "I'm going to kiss your cheek." "Look at this yellow book."
☆ This game is a great language developer.

When Will the Kisses Come?

Developmental milestone: Babies who are up to 3 months old may begin to respond to familiar voices.

☆ According to Jack Nitschke, a neuroscientist and assistant professor of psychiatry and psychology at the University of Wisconsin at Madison, when you speak to your baby in an animated voice, you are stimulating the orbitofrontal cortex of his brain, which is important in the development of attachment.
☆ To develop the orbitofrontal part of the brain, play this game with your baby.
☆ Say the following in an animated voice, accenting the beginning "F" sounds, "Fee, fi, fo, fum, when will the kisses come?" and then give your baby lots of kisses.
☆ Repeat, accenting the same sound or another beginning sound.

Bedtime Singing and Signing

Developmental milestone: Babies who are up to 3 months old may begin to respond to familiar voices.

⭐ There is no voice in the world that your baby likes more than yours. Sing him your favorite lullaby, or simply sing your favorite tune in a slow, soothing way.

⭐ Rock him or stand and gently sway as you sing. He will be relaxed but still awake.

⭐ Also sign the word *bed* as you tell him "Time for bed." (See sign on the right.) Your sweet song will become an important part of your bedtime ritual and help him to transition to slumber.

⭐ The sign for bed will also have more meaning If consistently paired with your special bedtime routines.

BED/SLEEP

High or Low?

Developmental milestone: Babies who are up to 3 months old may begin to respond to familiar voices.

⭐ Sit comfortably with your baby about 10 inches in front of you.

⭐ Call his name several times, using different voices from high to low.

⭐ Pause for a moment each time you say his name.

⭐ Watch his face for responses. Does he move or look at you intently when you use a high voice or a low voice? Does he kick his legs excitedly when you use a high voice or a low voice?

⭐ His responses will indicate which voice you should use with him.

Rhymes Are Fun

Developmental milestone: Babies who are up to 3 months old may begin to respond to familiar voices.

☆ Nursery rhymes are a wonderful way to introduce babies to rhythmic patterns, which present language in a way that is easy to understand.
☆ Pick your favorite rhymes, such as "One, Two, Buckle My Shoe" or "Jack and Jill."
☆ As you hold your baby close, say the rhymes and rock back and forth.

Talk to Me!

Developmental milestone: Babies who are up to 3 months old may begin to respond to familiar voices.

☆ Babies enjoy hearing the voices of the people around them.
☆ When you talk to a baby, you stimulate the development of the hearing center in the brain. The longer and more you talk with your baby, the more neuron-to-neuron connections occur. According to Dr. Barbara Davis and Dr. Peter MacNeilage of the University of Texas at Austin, these connections at the hearing center of the brain build a foundation for a baby's first word.
☆ Use everyday experiences as opportunities to talk with your baby. For example, when you are changing his diaper, describe what you are doing. Show him the diaper. Smile and say, "This is your diaper. I am going to put it on you." When you are finished changing his diaper, say, "All done!" Or when you are bathing him, describe what you are doing.
☆ How you speak to your baby, including the words and inflections

you use, is also important. Here are a few ideas:

o Change the tone and volume of your voice for emphasis.

o Speak slowly. Pause between each phrase or short sentence.

o Give your baby a chance to "talk" to you with his eyes by being quiet for a minute or two.

o Repeat words or phrases. For example, say, "I am going to give you a bath" in a voice that shows enthusiasm. Emphasize the word "bath." Say, "A bath is so much fun!" continuing to show enthusiasm and emphasizing the word "bath." When you place your baby in the water, say, "The water in the bath feels so nice" in a soft, gentle voice still emphasizing the word "bath."

Ah, Boo!

Developmental milestone: Babies who are up to 3 months old may begin to respond to familiar voices.

☆ Babies who develop a strong attachment to their daily caregivers, which includes both parents and caregivers, are likely to develop into happy and secure children.

☆ The following is an enjoyable way to foster intimacy and attachment: Hold your baby at eye level and touch his forehead to yours very gently. As you touch foreheads, say, "Ah, boo!"

☆ When you say "Boo," move your forehead away from your baby's forehead and smile at him.

☆ You can also extend the word "ah" to "ahhhhhh."

☆ Your baby will love this game, and you will love the connections between you and your baby that the game creates.

Follow the Colors

Developmental milestone: Babies who are up to 3 months old may stare at objects or faces of people.

☆ A baby's visual range is limited at birth. The colors that babies see are also limited. At first, the colors that they see best are red, white, and black.
☆ Draw black and red shapes on white paper or a white paper plate.
☆ Your baby will delight in looking at these shapes.
☆ Slowly move the plate in different directions so that your baby can follow the colors.

Bright Colors

Developmental milestone: Babies who are up to 3 months old may stare at objects or faces of people.

☆ Include in the environment brightly colored objects and toys.
☆ Your baby will enjoy looking at these objects.
☆ Brightly colored toys or toys with contrasting colors will stimulate his brain.

Happy Face Peek-a-Boo

Developmental milestone: Babies who are up to 3 months old may stare at objects or faces of people.

☆ This peek-a-boo game makes babies more aware of faces. It also introduces the concept of front and back.
☆ Draw a face on the front of a white paper plate. You can also paste a picture of a face on the plate.

☆ Hold the face in front of your baby at a comfortable distance and say, "Happy face, happy face."

☆ Now show your baby the back of the plate with nothing on it.

☆ Turn the plate back and say, "Peek-a-boo baby!" in an enthusiastic voice.

☆ Repeat until your baby tires of the experience.

Beginning Bonding

EAT

Developmental milestone: Babies who are up to 3 months old may stare at objects or faces of people.

☆ Using sign language with babies at this stage helps them learn to focus on the face and hands of the person making the sign.

☆ Practice making signs and then use signs with your baby. It will enhance your baby's conversation skills and your ability and confidence to use signs.

BED/SLEEP

☆ The combination of your voice, facial expressions, and hand motions will fascinate your child, and nurture the love that is blossoming between you.

☆ When you say "eat" or "sleep," accompany the words with the signs to "talk" about your baby's two basic needs.

Note: Once your baby begins to use the sign for the word *sleep* (typically at around 9 months to 1 year of age), he may place one or both hands on his head and tap several times. He may also use the sign for "tired" as well, as their meanings are interchangeable to a young child.

I Can Do It Too!

Developmental milestone: Babies who are up to 3 months old may stare at objects or faces of people.

☆ Babies love to mimic your changing facial expressions.
☆ With both of your hands supporting your baby's back and head, bring your face about 10 inches from his eyes.
☆ Blink your eyes. Repeat several times, pausing each time.
☆ Notice if he blinks his eyes.
☆ Try sticking out your tongue and see if he will copy you.
☆ The mirroring in this game develops your baby's self-awareness.

Look into My Eyes

Developmental milestone: Babies who are up to 3 months old may stare at objects or faces of people.

☆ When your newborn's eyes are open, move your face close to his and look into his eyes.
☆ Each time he looks at you, he is developing his memory skills.
☆ As you look into his eyes, softly speak a few words.

Rock Your Baby

Developmental milestone: Babies who are up to 3 months old may react to and be comforted by many kinds of sounds.

☆ Gently rock your baby to the sounds of soothing music.
☆ Hold your baby and dance slowly with him.
☆ This type of movement is very soothing because it is similar to what he experienced in the womb.

Rhythmic Sounds

Developmental milestone: Babies who are up to 3 months old may react to and be comforted by many kinds of sounds.

- ☆ Music and rhythmic sounds are comforting to newborn babies.
- ☆ Noises such as a vacuum cleaner or a car engine have been known to be calming to some babies.
- ☆ It is said that these sounds may be linked to infants' recollections of the comfort of hearing their mothers' heartbeats in the womb.
- ☆ Try different sounds to see what soothes your baby. Some sounds that you could try are singing a melody with the word "la," snapping your fingers, or clicking your tongue.

Nurturing Rituals

Developmental milestone: Babies who are up to 3 months old may react to and be comforted by many kinds of sounds.

- ☆ Nurturing rituals make your baby feel secure while developing your baby's sense of trust (knowing that the same thing will happen each day).
- ☆ Nurture your baby by touching, talking to, smiling at, or singing to him when you are feeding, diapering, or bathing him.

Soothing Music

Developmental milestone: Babies who are up to 3 months old may react to and be comforted by many kinds of sounds.

☆ Playing classical music for your baby (or for you) is a lovely experience.

☆ Many researchers believe that babies can hear from about 7 months in utero.

☆ Most babies and young children are calmed by lullabies.

☆ Sing a lullaby every night and you will calm your baby and create a bond that will last forever.

I Love Your Face!

Developmental milestone: Babies who are up to 3 months old may smile at faces.

☆ Faces are very interesting and babies will delight in exploring your face, especially if the mouth on your face is making all sorts of funny noises and shapes!

☆ Move your face close to your baby's so he can reach out and grab your nose.

Bumblebee, Bumblebee

Developmental milestone: Babies who are up to 3 months old may like when people or objects touch their skin.

☆ This is a good game to play at diaper-changing time.
☆ Take your index finger and make a circle in the air. Come closer and closer to your baby as you say, "Bumblebee, bumblebee, straight from the farm—buzz, buzz, buzz under your arm."
☆ Make a buzzing sound and nuzzle your baby under the arm.

Up and Down My Back

Developmental milestone: Babies who are up to 3 months old may like when people or objects touch their skin.

☆ Place your baby on his back on the floor.
☆ Take a small, soft ball and roll it up and down his body.
☆ Now turn him on his tummy and roll the ball up and down his back.
☆ You can also roll the ball in a circular motion on both his back and his tummy.
☆ This is a very pleasant experience for your baby.

Gentle Touch

Developmental milestone: Babies who are up to 3 months old may like when people or objects touch their skin.

☆ Touch is a very important sense that impacts babies' cognitive development, sociability, ability to withstand stress, and immunological development. According to www.johnsonbaby.com, infants who are handled gently and carefully, as opposed to being tickled or poked, spend more time making eye contact, smiling, and vocalizing and less time crying.

☆ Although most infants enjoy gentle touching, preferences will vary from infant to infant.

☆ Explore different types of touch, such as stroking, bouncing, and so on, to see which types of touch your baby prefers.

☆ It is also good to take your baby's hand and stroke it on your face. Experiences that have an element of touch help develop a bond with your baby.

Soft Air

Developmental milestone: Babies who are up to 3 months old may like when people or objects touch their skin.

☆ An interesting way to touch your baby is to use a straw and blow your warm breath on different parts of his body.

☆ Blow on your baby's arm and say, "I am blowing on your arm." Blow on his tummy and say, "I am blowing on your tummy."

☆ This game helps your baby begin to learn about the different parts of his body.

Hugging, Snuggling, and Kissing

Developmental milestone: Babies who are up to 3 months old may like when people or objects touch their skin.

✫ Hugging, snuggling, and kissing stimulate your baby's senses.
✫ When your baby feels the warmth of a human body next to his, he develops a sense of security and confidence to try new things.

Milk Sign

Developmental milestone: Babies who are up to 3 months old may like when people or objects touch their skin.

✫ Use the sign for *milk* to refer to either mother's milk or formula. This is an important sign because milk is the only source of nutrition for babies at this stage.
✫ Hold your baby in your arms and show him the *milk* sign as you say the word "milk."
✫ Ask him if he wants milk as you gently cup your hand around his to give his hand a gentle squeeze. This gentle motion is how your child first experiences sign language: by feeling your hands on his shaping the gestures.
✫ Provide milk for your baby after you say and sign the word so that he learns that the word *milk* is what you call his favorite food group!
✫ Use this sign whenever you say the word *milk.*
  Note: Once your baby begins to use the sign (typically at around 9 months to 1 year of age), he may imitate your sign for *milk* by opening and closing his hand several times.

MILK

Games and Experiences to Develop Babies' Intellectual/Thinking Skills

I Love My Hand!

Developmental milestone: Babies who are up to 3 months old may discover their hands and feet.

☆ At about 2 months, your baby may begin to look at his hand for a sustained period of time. Some experts call this "hand regard."

☆ Use a nontoxic marker to draw a simple black-and-white pattern on a mitten.

☆ If you put this mitten on his hand he may stare at it longer than a mitten without a pattern.

Jack in the Box

Developmental milestone: Babies who are up to 3 months old may discover their hands and feet.

☆ The following is a playful way to interact with your baby.

☆ When you have your baby's attention, make a fist with your right hand and hide your thumb inside. Say, "Jack in the box, Jack in the box."

☆ Knock on your fist with your other hand and say, "Wake up, wake up! Someone is knocking, knock, knock, knock!"

☆ Pop your thumb out from inside your fist and say, "Hello, Jack, how are you?"

☆ Repeat, moving his hands to the words.

☆ Moving your baby's fingers and thumbs is a good way to develop his fine motor skills.

Socks on My Hands, Socks on My Feet

Developmental milestone: Babies who are up to 3 months old may discover their hands and feet.

☆ Put colored socks on baby's hands and feet.
☆ The bright colors of the socks will engage your baby's interest. He will look at the colors of the socks and may try to put the socks in his mouth.
☆ A sock with a pattern is also wonderful for stimulating your baby's vision.

Five Fingers

Developmental milestone: Babies who are up to 3 months old may discover their hands and feet.

☆ Say the following as you hold and kiss each individual finger.
  Thumbkin (thumb)
  Peter-Pointer (index finger)
  Long and Lanky (middle finger)
  Hanky-Panky (ring finger)
  Pinky-Pinky-Pinky-Winky (smallest finger)
☆ Say, "All done!" and then take your baby's hand and kiss it.

Reach for the Toy

Developmental milestone: Babies who are up to 3 months old may discover their hands and feet.

- ☆ Place your baby on his back.
- ☆ Hold a brightly colored toy over his chest within his reach.
- ☆ Encourage him to reach up to get the toy.
- ☆ He will delight in bringing the toy closer to his face to study it better.

Tap a Rhythm

Developmental milestone: Babies who are up to 3 months old may discover their hands and feet.

- ☆ This experience helps your baby "feel" a simple rhythm.
- ☆ According to Jessica Phillips-Silver and Laurel J. Trainor in *Feeling the Beat*, babies experience music using one or more of their senses. For example, babies might hear the words and feel the beat.
- ☆ Place your baby on his back in a place that is safe.
- ☆ Alternately, gently tap the bottoms of your baby's feet to any song with a simple rhythm such as "Twinkle, Twinkle, Little Star."

Touch and Feel

Developmental milestone: Babies who are up to 3 months old may enjoy feeling different textures.

☆ Provide interesting objects for your baby to feel, touch, mouth, and explore.

☆ Guide your baby's hand to touch common household items, such as soft scarves, cold metal bowls, and wet washcloths. As your baby develops, he can learn to do this on his own.

Who Is It?

Developmental milestone: Babies who are up to 3 months old may recognize familiar faces and scents.

☆ Sit your baby in an infant seat and then sit directly in front of him.

☆ Put a hat on your head, such as a baseball cap, a clown hat, or even a pair of ear muffs.

☆ Take the hat off and say, "Look, it's me!" Repeat several times.

☆ Lean forward toward your baby and see if he wants to try to pull off the hat.

A World of Smells

Developmental milestone: Babies who are up to 3 months old may recognize familiar faces and scents.

* A baby's sense of smell is well developed at birth. Within hours after birth, babies respond much like adults to a variety of odors. For example, infants prefer and smile at odors like bananas and vanilla.
* Infants soon begin to develop preferences for certain smells. They prefer the smell of their mothers to the smell of other women.
* Studies, such as the one by Cindy McGaha of Appalachian State University, show that infants select and manipulate a vanilla-scented toy more frequently than unscented toys.
* Your baby's reaction to smells will help you learn what he finds pleasant. Note whether your baby smiles and coos in response to a scent or turns his head away.
* Use your baby's preferences for certain smells to make experiences and objects more engaging for infants. If a toy is scented with an odor that is pleasing to your infant, he will want to touch it, grasp it, and investigate it in many ways.

Left and Right

Developmental milestone: Babies who are up to 3 months old may be aware of their left and right sides.

* Developing an awareness of left and right can begin at a very early age.
* Place your baby face down on a blanket on the floor. Use his name in a sentence, such as "Hi, Nathan! You have bright blue eyes."

☆ If he raises his head, repeat the same words on the left side of his face, then in front of him, and then on the right side of his face.

☆ Gently turn him over on his back and repeat, starting on the left side again.

Arms and Legs

Developmental milestone: Babies who are up to 3 months old may be aware of their left and right sides.

☆ When your baby is on his back, take his left arm and gently stretch it out to the side. Now do the same to his right arm. If he keeps his arms out to the side, it means that he is aware of his arms. If they curl back, he hasn't developed awareness yet.

☆ Do the same with your baby's legs. Starting on the left side, move the leg out to the side. Always start with the left and then the right. (This is a very subtle way to introduce the fact that we read from the left to the right.)

☆ As you are doing this, describe what you are doing. For example, "I am moving your left arm out to the side."

My Favorite Sound

Developmental milestone: Babies who are up to 3 months old may begin to connect sounds with their sources.

☆ A newborn's favorite sound is the human voice.

☆ Talk with your baby about what you see around you and what you are doing. "Now I'm going to take off your wet diaper." "I see a red ball on the floor."

☆ The more words a baby hears, the more vocabulary he will develop.

Sounds I Like

Developmental milestone: Babies who are up to 3 months old may begin to connect sounds with their sources.

☆ Notice the kind of sounds your baby likes best.
☆ Some infants love music with strong beats, while others prefer softer melodies.
☆ Don't be shy about singing. No matter how in or out of tune you sing, your baby will like your voice best of all.
☆ Vary your voice from high pitches to low pitches and from fast speech to slow speech. Explore additional sounds you can produce.
☆ Notice your baby's response when you crumple or tear paper, knock on a door or floor, turn on the faucet, turn on the washing machine, or make other familiar sounds.

Jingle the Bells

Developmental milestone: Babies who are up to 3 months old may begin to connect sounds with their sources.

☆ The following develops your baby's auditory awareness in addition to being a lovely bonding experience.
   Note: You will need some jingle bells to play this game.
☆ Hold your baby in your arms and jingle the bells near his face.
☆ When you are sure that he is listening to the sound, move the bells to the left side of his face and jingle them again.
☆ If he does not move his head to follow the sound, you can move it for him.

☆ Repeat, jingling the bells back and forth first on the left and then on the right. When you feel that he is able to identify where the sound is, jingle them up above his head to encourage him to lift his head upward toward the sound.

Songs and Rhymes

Developmental milestone: Babies who are up to 3 months old may distinguish different voices, qualities, and tone.

☆ From time to time throughout the day, sing or recite a poem.

☆ Hold your baby so he can watch your face.

☆ Pick a song or rhyme that enables you to use your baby's name. For example, If you sing "Do You know the Muffin Man?" substitute "muffin man" with your baby's name.

☆ Other suggestions include "This Old Man," "Itsy Bitsy Spider," and "Little Miss Muffet."

2 FOR BABIES 3–6 MONTHS OLD

Physical Development

Babies who are 3–6 months old may

☆ Wiggle forward on the floor
☆ Roll over in both directions
☆ Grab an object that is near their hands
☆ Grasp a toy
☆ Hold their head up for a long time without bobbing
☆ Play with their hands and feet
☆ Be aware of many sounds
☆ Be aware of their arms and legs

Social-Emotional Development

Babies who are 3–6 months old may

☆ Babble ("ba-ba")
☆ Gurgle, coo, and squeal
☆ Respond to verbal cues
☆ Watch as you move your mouth
☆ Study faces
☆ Respond to experiences that stimulate their senses
☆ Like to play
☆ Smile responsively
☆ Like social interaction

Intellectual Development

Babies who are 3–6 months old may

☆ Be aware that people and things have labels ("Dada")
☆ Be developing memory
☆ Be aware of their environment
☆ Begin to understand taking turns

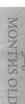

Games and Experiences to Develop Babies' Physical Skills

Crawling

Developmental milestone: Babies who are 3–6 months old may wiggle forward on the floor.

☆ This experience gives your baby practice for crawling.

☆ Place your baby on her tummy on a carpeted or nonslippery floor surface.

☆ Place one of her favorite toys on the ground a few inches from her head.

☆ Press your hands against her feet. Your baby will push against the pressure, causing her to move forward a few inches toward the toy.

☆ Keep moving the toy and pushing against her feet.

☆ Before you know it, she will be half way across the room!

Get That Toy!

Developmental milestone: Babies who are 3–6 months old may wiggle forward on the floor.

☆ Give your baby time on her tummy so she can exercise her neck muscles and begin to reach for objects in an attempt to crawl.

☆ While she is on her tummy, put a toy in front of her so that she can reach out to get the toy. Try several different toys and let her be successful in reaching them.

☆ Next, put the toy just a little out of reach so that she will have to move to get the toy. If it is too hard for her, then physically move her to the toy.

☆ This game develops your baby's coordination.

Exercise, Exercise

Developmental milestone: Babies who are 3–6 months old may wiggle forward on the floor.

☆ Place your baby on her back and place your thumbs in her palms. When she has a solid grip on your thumbs, bend and straighten her arms while she remains on her back. As you do this, say, "Exercise, exercise, it's such fun to exercise."

☆ Place your thumbs on the soles of your baby's feet. After she curls her toes around your thumbs, slowly bicycle her legs in the air. Repeat "Exercise, exercise, it's such fun to exercise."

☆ These activities help develop your baby's motor skills.

Roll Over, Roll Over!

Developmental milestone: Babies who are 3–6 months old may roll over in both directions.

☆ This exercise helps your baby begin to roll over.

☆ Place your baby on her tummy on a soft blanket.

☆ Slowly and carefully pick up one side of the blanket until your baby tilts a little to the side.

☆ Continue slowly rolling your baby over while you describe what she is doing. Use your hand to help guide her.
Note: Be sure to support your baby's head as she rolls to her back.

☆ When she has turned over completely, clap your hands in delight.

Soft and Silky

Developmental milestone: Babies who are 3–6 months old may roll over in both directions.

☆ This relaxing game gives your baby a very nice tactile experience.
☆ Place your baby on her back and cover her tummy with a soft silk scarf. Say words that describe the texture, such as "This feels so good" or "soft and smooth for baby (use child's name)."
☆ Turn her over on her tummy and do the same thing on her back.

Soft Colors

Developmental milestone: Babies who are 3–6 months old may grab an object that is near their hands.

☆ Place a colorful scarf through a bracelet that is safe for a baby to handle.
☆ Tie the scarf to a sturdy piece of furniture.
☆ Place your baby near the bracelet and scarf so she can grab the bracelet and move the scarf around.
☆ This develops her eye-hand coordination.

Open, Shut Them

Developmental milestone: Babies who are 3–6 months old may grasp a toy.

☆ This game helps your baby gain control of her hands when she grasps a toy.
☆ While your baby is sitting in a highchair, place a graspable toy in front of her.

☆ Encourage her to take the toy and after she has held it for a few minutes, gently open her fingers and remove the toy.

☆ Take her hand and open and close it as you say, "Open, shut them, open, shut them, very, very good."

Pony Ride

Developmental milestone: Babies who are 3–6 months old may hold their head up for a long time without bobbing.

☆ As your baby increases her neck strength and head control, take her on some pony rides.

☆ Place a small, soft blanket or towel over one of your knees.

☆ Seat your baby on your knee facing you. Hold her securely.

☆ Gently move your knee up and down so that she will experience a bounce.

☆ Ask your baby, "Shall we bounce?" and then say, "Okay, let's ride the pony." As you bounce, say, "Wheee."

Jingle Feet

Developmental milestone: Babies who are 3–6 months old may play with their hands and feet.

☆ Place socks with jingle bells on the toes on your baby's feet.

☆ Place your baby on her back and chant the following to her as you gently lift her left leg toward her face. "Jingle bells, left foot, jingle bells, left foot."

☆ Put her left leg down and then gently move her right foot toward her face as you say the same words using "right foot" instead of "left foot."

☆ After doing this several times, remove the socks and wiggle her toes one by one. As you wiggle her toes, say, "Wiggle, wiggle."

Listen to the Sound

Developmental milestone: Babies who are 3–6 months old may be aware of many sounds.

☆ Introduce your baby to new sounds by making the sound and then identifying it.

☆ Say, "Listen to the sound," make the sound, and then say what it is.

☆ Here are some ideas: Tap a pencil on different surfaces, tap a spoon on a glass, bounce a ball, clap your hands together, snap your fingers, whistle, turn on a water faucet, play a musical instrument, listen to different styles and rhythms of music, and so on.

Sounds Are All Around

Developmental milestone: Babies who are 3–6 months old may be aware of many sounds.

☆ An infant's hearing develops rapidly during the first 12 months. Infants are born with the ability to discriminate between sounds (an important foundation for language), and this ability continues to develop.

☆ Babies soon begin to show a preference for the sounds of their own language. The conversations that you have with babies and that they hear you have with other people contribute to the development of their language skills.

☆ Think of three nursery rhymes or songs and recite or sing them daily.

☆ When your baby is older, she will begin to sing them with you. When she is older, if you leave out a word you will find that your baby will fill it in.

Through Your Toes

Developmental milestone: Babies who are 3–6 months old may be aware of their arms and legs.

- ☆ Use lots of touch on your baby's hands and feet. You can rub them with cotton, wool, silk, fur, and other fabrics.
- ☆ Pull a soft ribbon through her toes and fingers.
- ☆ This experience helps her become aware that her hands and feet are connected to her body.

Up and Down

Developmental milestone: Babies who are 3–6 months old may be aware of their arms and legs.

- ☆ Stretch your arms out in front of you with your baby face down on your arms and her feet pressing against your chest.
- ☆ Move around the room, carefully lowering and raising your arms as you sing a song such as "Twinkle, Twinkle, Little Star."
- ☆ Lie down on your back and place her face down on your chest.
- ☆ Say, "One, two, three and up we go" as you raise her in the air while singing the same song.
- ☆ As she raises her head, she will be strengthening her neck muscles.

Games and Experiences to Develop Babies' Social-Emotional Skills

The Art of Conversation

Developmental milestone: Babies who are 3–6 months old may babble ("ba-ba").

☆ Pay attention to the rhythm of your baby's babble and you will discover that she babbles a bit and then pauses. She pauses because she is waiting for you to respond to her.

☆ Respond by mimicking her babble or saying a few words. Then pause.

☆ Wait for your baby to babble again.

☆ This teaches the art of conversation.

☆ Try it! You will be amazed.

Babbling

Developmental milestone: Babies who are 3–6 months old may babble ("ba-ba").

☆ When babies begin to make babbling sounds, they often start with the sounds that the letters "P," "B," and "M" make.

☆ Say words that begin with these sounds to help your baby develop her language skills.

☆ Sing songs, changing all the beginning sounds in each word to the same letter sound. For example, instead of singing "Mary had a little lamb," sing "Bary bad a bittle bamb."

☆ Engage in a "conversation" with your baby using the same sound over and over.

☆ According to Dr. Alan Greene (www.drgreene.com), research confirms that babbling is an important sign of good language development.

Mousie, Mousie

Developmental milestone: Babies who are 3–6 months old may like to play.

☆ This is a great activity to do at diaper-changing time.
☆ Begin by walking your fingers up your baby's leg while saying "mousie, mousie, mousie."
☆ When you come to her tummy, stop, and then say the words again very quickly.
☆ Play the game again and start at your baby's arm and walk your fingers toward her head. Stop short and then say the words again very quickly.
☆ Your baby will soon learn that when you stop, she will hear the words very quickly.
☆ This helps babies learn to focus their attention on what is happening.

Scampering

Developmental milestone: Babies who are 3–6 months old may like to play.

☆ Hold your baby in your arms.
☆ Hold up three fingers and bounce them on your baby's palm as you say the following words. "See these little mice? They are going to scamper up your arm."
☆ When you say "scamper," wiggle your fingers up and down your baby's arm.
☆ Repeat with a different part of the body. For example, "See these little mice? They are going to scamper on your tummy." Scamper on your baby's nose, leg, cheek, and so on.

Parentese

Developmental milestone: Babies who are 3–6 months old may gurgle, coo, and squeal.

☆ Speaking in "parentese" is using a high voice, drawing out vowels, and changing the tone of your voice. Speak to your baby in simple sentences, drawing out the last word of each line.
  ○ You have very pretty haaaaair.
  ○ Your eyes are bluuuuuuue.
  ○ I love youuuuuuu.
☆ Your baby will respond with coos and smiles.

Finger Puppet

Developmental milestone: Babies who are 3–6 months old may gurgle, coo, and squeal.

☆ Put a puppet on your finger and dance it up and down and back and forth.
☆ Make the puppet talk to your baby. "I'm going to give you a kiss." "You're a nice baby."
☆ Your baby's response to the puppet will help develop her visual skills.

Make a Funny Face

Developmental milestone: Babies who are 3–6 months old may gurgle, coo, and squeal.

☆ Make a funny face or stick out your tongue. You will see that she will do the same. Your newborn is quite perceptive!
☆ This is your baby's first attempt at a reciprocal social interaction.
☆ Do the following and see if your baby will try to copy you.
　○ Make a funny sound.
　○ Purse your lips.
　○ Stick out your tongue.
　○ Open and close your eyes.

Coo and Squeal

Developmental milestone: Babies who are 3–6 months old may gurgle, coo, and squeal.

☆ When infants see something that is interesting to them, they react. Sometimes they react by cooing and squealing.
☆ Make a cooing sound to your baby and wait for her to respond. When she does, return the sound.
☆ When your baby gets a response to her sound, she will make those sounds again and again.
☆ This develops early language skills.

Early Communication

Developmental milestone: Babies who are 3–6 months old may gurgle, coo, and squeal.

☆ Encourage your baby to begin to make sounds.

☆ Slowly move a brightly colored scarf in the air in front of your baby.

☆ When your baby responds with a delighted coo (or another sound), answer her by repeating her sound.

☆ Experiment with different objects so you learn what she likes.

☆ This will help develop early communications skills.

You Are Special

Developmental milestone: Babies who are 3–6 months old may smile responsively.

☆ Building your baby's self-esteem starts at birth. By the time a baby is 3–4 months old, there are many things you can do to make her feel proud of her accomplishments.

☆ When your baby grabs your finger, responds by cooing, or rolls over, say something that recognizes her accomplishments, such as "I feel your strong hand holding my finger," "I hear you talking," or "You rolled over!"

☆ Because babies thrive in an environment where they feel a strong bond with the adults in their lives, kiss your baby's fingertips and put her fingertips on your lips.

This Is What I Am Going to Do

Developmental milestone: Babies who are 3–6 months old may respond to verbal cues.

☆ Always tell your baby what you are going to do before you do it. Here are some examples:
- Say, "I'm going to pick you up," and then hold out your arms.
- Say, "I'm going to change your diaper," and then place your baby on her back.
- Say, "I'm going to kiss you," and then pucker up your lips.

☆ Soon your baby will begin to understand the language and you will only have to say one or two words for her to respond by imitating your actions or facial expressions.

☆ This approach helps babies internalize the meaning and importance of language.

Hello and Goodbye

Developmental milestone: Babies who are 3–6 months old may respond to verbal cues.

☆ This game will teach your baby the meaning of the words "hello" and "goodbye."

☆ When you enter a room and see your baby, say "Hello" with a big smile on your face. Now leave the room and say "Goodbye" and wave your hand.

☆ Wait a moment, come back and say "Hello" again.

☆ Repeat this and, over time, your baby will learn the meaning of these two words.

Rocking

Developmental milestone: Babies who are 3–6 months old may like social interaction.

☆ Rocking games help babies develop their sense of balance.

☆ Sit on the floor, holding your baby on your legs. Her back should be resting against your chest.

☆ Cuddle your child and slowly rock back and forth several times. Then rock from side to side several times.

☆ Keep repeating the rocking motion as you sing a favorite song.

Swaying

Developmental milestone: Babies who are 3–6 months old may like social interaction.

☆ Games such as the following stimulate your baby's vestibular or balance system.

☆ Hold your baby on your hip and slowly sway from side to side as you listen to soft and gentle music.

☆ Continue swaying as you move your body in different ways. As you sway, you can lift your feet, turn in a circle, or step sideways, forward, and backward.

☆ This will help your baby feel the movement throughout her body. You can also experiment with different ways to hold your baby.

Who Are You?

Developmental milestone: Babies who are 3–6 months old may like social interaction.

☆ Babies love this game because they enjoy watching the expressions on your face and suddenly realizing who you are.
☆ Put on a hat and a scarf.
☆ Move toward your baby while singing a song.
☆ As you sing, slowly take off the hat and the scarf.
☆ Your baby will be happy hearing the music and even happier when she recognizes who you are.

Copy Cat

Developmental milestone: Babies who are 3–6 months old may watch as you move your mouth.

☆ Hold your baby in your lap facing you so she can see your face clearly.
☆ Make different noises with your mouth and encourage your baby to copy you.
☆ Some ideas to try are kissing, clicking your tongue, blowing your lips like a motor boat, and making a "raspberry" sound with your tongue.
☆ Facial expressions are contagious. If your baby yawns, she may make you yawn!

Feel the Sound

Developmental milestone: Babies who are 3–6 months old may watch as you move your mouth.

* ☆ Place your baby's fingers on your lips as you make different consonant and vowel sounds: /b/, /m/, /d/, "ah," "ee," and "oo."
* ☆ When you let her feel the vibrations while you make each sound, you increase her interest in language.

Hand Face

Developmental milestone: Babies who are 3–6 months old may study faces.

* ☆ Use a nontoxic marker to draw a face on the pad of each of your fingers and both thumbs.
* ☆ Make a fist and then open your fingers so your baby can see the faces on your fingers. As you do this, say the words "open" and "shut."
* ☆ Open each finger at a time. Say "hello" to that finger and then close it. For example: open your thumb and say "hello." Wiggle your thumb and then close it. Continue on with each finger.
* ☆ Your baby will be fascinated with the faces on your fingers. She will also begin to copy you and open and close her fingers.

From Babbling to Words

Developmental milestone: Babies who are 3–6 months old may study faces.

* ☆ According to researchers Alison Gopnik and Thierry Nazzi, the babbling sounds that babies make are not random sounds strung

together but instead are what babies do to learn how to move their lips, tongues, mouths, and jaws to make the sounds they hear.

☆ As your baby babbles, move closer to her so your face is comfortably in her visual range and babble back to her.

☆ She will watch your face very carefully. As you babble back and forth (always pause after you babble or say or few words), add one word to your babbling. For example, "baby." As she watches your mouth move and hears the sounds, she will begin to learn the word.

☆ On another day or at another time, add a new word after repeating the old words first.

Glove Face

Developmental milestone: Babies who are 3–6 months old may study faces.

☆ This experience builds on the fact that infants like to look at faces.

☆ Cut the fingers off a pair of solid-color knit gloves.

☆ Use a bright-colored, nontoxic marker to draw a colorful face in the middle of the palm of the glove.

☆ Put the glove on your hand.

☆ Hold your baby in your lap.

☆ Show your baby your hand. You can wiggle your fingers, make your glove face "talk," sing songs and move the glove face to the song, or use the glove to tell stories.

☆ Your little one will be fascinated as she develops her social skills.

Facial Expressions

Developmental milestone: Babies who are 3–6 months old may study faces.

☆ Hold your baby so she can see your face.
☆ Make one or two of the following expressions:
- ○ Smile
- ○ Stick out your tongue.
- ○ Show your teeth, point to them and say "teeth."
- ○ Pull your ears as you say "ear."
- ○ Make different sounds by shaping your lips in different ways.

☆ If your baby starts to copy you, repeat the expression or sound she made.
☆ This is wonderful for developing observation skills and bonding.

Floating Feathers

Developmental milestone: Babies who are 3–6 months old may respond to experiences that stimulate their senses.

☆ Lie down on your back with your baby next to you.
☆ Throw a brightly colored feather in the air and watch it gently float to the ground.
☆ This is a very relaxing game to play and it also challenges your baby to follow (track) objects with her eyes.
Note: You can find feathers at art supply stores.

Hear the Sound

Developmental milestone: Babies who are 3–6 months old may respond to experiences that stimulate their senses.

☆ This game awakens your baby's sense of sound.

☆ Take a set of keys or jingle bells and slowly swing them back and forth in front of your baby so she can follow your actions.

☆ Speak to your baby about the sounds: "Listen to the jingly bells." "Oh, I like the bell sound."

☆ Place your baby's hand on yours as you jingle the bells back and forth and say the words.

Feel the Touch

Developmental milestone: Babies who are 3–6 months old may respond to experiences that stimulate their senses.

☆ Babies simply love to be touched. It's an important part of their growth and development. Skin-to-skin contact creates a special bonding between you and your baby.

☆ Expand your baby's sense of touch by letting her experience being touched by other materials.

☆ Take a piece of fur and gently rub it along her arm. Describe the experience for her by saying, "This feels so soft," or "Oh, doesn't that feel nice on your arm!"

☆ Repeat with other fabrics like felt, silk, or terrycloth. Describe the different touch sensation that each fabric presents to your baby.

A Touching Game

Developmental milestone: Babies who are 3–6 months old may respond to experiences that stimulate their senses.

☆ This touching game stimulates your baby's senses and begins to lay the foundation for understanding left and right, a key component of learning how to read.

☆ Place your baby on her back and stroke her left arm. As you stroke her arm, say soothing words like "sweet baby" or "I love you." Continue by stroking her right arm.

☆ Move to the left leg and then the right leg. Turn your baby on her tummy and repeat the stroking, first left, then right.

☆ Now pick up your baby and kiss her on her left cheek and then her right cheek.

☆ If you continue to do the left side first, when your child starts to read, she will be comfortable with the concept of reading from left to right.

Games and Experiences to Develop Babies' Intellectual/Thinking Skills

Where Is Baby's Arm?

Developmental milestone: Babies who are 3–6 months old may be aware that people and things have labels ("Dada").

☆ Boost your baby's language skills by describing what you are doing. According to Erika Hoff-Ginsberg in *Language Development*, talking with your baby while you dress and feed her provides just what she needs to learn to communicate.

☆ As you dress your baby, say the following as you do the actions described. "Where's the baby's arm? Here's the baby's arm. Shake it up and shake it down. Put it in the shirt."

☆ Repeat using different parts of the body, such as baby's leg, baby's elbow, baby's head, and so on.

Kitchen Words

Developmental milestone: Babies who are 3–6 months old may be aware that people and things have labels ("Dada").

☆ When you are in your kitchen, show your baby different items that you are using, such as an unbreakable dish.

☆ Say "dish" several times and then let her touch the dish with your help.

☆ Move the dish up and down slowly and from side to side as you repeat the word "dish."

☆ Repeat this game with other kitchen items, such as fruits, vegetables, silverware, and so on. Always say the word many times as you do the movements.
Safety note: Be sure all items that you give your baby are safe for her to handle.

How Signing Feels

Developmental milestone: Babies who are 3–6 months old may be developing memory.

☆ You can help your baby learn to sign. Gently place your hands on your baby's and shape the signs using her hands and fingers so she learns what the signs feel like.

☆ Over time, she will figure out that these motions are purposeful, not random, movements and can help her communicate what she wants and needs.

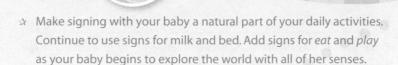

☆ Make signing with your baby a natural part of your daily activities. Continue to use signs for milk and bed. Add signs for *eat* and *play* as your baby begins to explore the world with all of her senses.

Sign for eat: Tap gathered fingertips to lips. Once your baby begins to use the sign (typically at around 9 months to 1 year of age), she may place her open hand on or in her mouth.

Sign for play: Extend thumb and little fingers of both closed fists and twist both at wrists. Once your baby begins to use the sign (typically at around 9 months to 1 year of age), she may shake both of her open hands repetitively.

EAT

PLAY

Where Is the Toy?

Developmental milestone: Babies who are 3–6 months old may be developing memory.

☆ Watch how your baby reacts when things disappear from her view. Does she lean over to look for things she dropped? Does she put a toy down and go back to it later?

☆ These are signs that your baby's memory is starting to develop. When she was younger, it was "out of sight, out of mind." Now she is learning that things exist even when not in sight.

☆ Show your baby a favorite toy, then turn her away so she can't see it. If she turns her head or body to look for the toy, help her get the toy and say encouraging words to her such as "That was fun, let's do it again."

Peek-a-Boo Toy

Developmental milestone: Babies who are 3–6 months old may be developing memory.

☆ Sit down and place your baby in your lap.
☆ Put a toy in your hands. Play with the toy.
☆ Take a scarf or towel and cover the toy.
☆ If your baby tries to pull the cover off, it means that she remembers where it is. If she doesn't remember, pull the cover off and say, "Peek-a-boo toy."
☆ Play this several times to develop your baby's memory.

Look at the Light

Developmental milestone: Babies who are 3–6 months old may be aware of their environment.

☆ This game enhances your baby's visual skills.
☆ Sit on a comfortable chair in a dark room with your baby in your lap.
☆ Shine a flashlight on the wall to get your baby's attention. Then say something to your baby such as, "Look at the pretty light." As you say the words, slowly move the flashlight up and down so that the light moves.
☆ As you move the flashlight around, let it stop on familiar objects. If it's a table, say, "There's a table."
☆ Continue shining the light on other objects in the room until your baby grows tired of the game.

Sharing a Meal

Developmental milestone: Babies who are 3–6 months old may begin to understand taking turns.

☆ Babies this age discover that they aren't the only ones who enjoy eating food.

☆ Make snack time or mealtime a social activity and serve yourself a helping of whatever you are feeding your child. Sign *eat* as you say, "I am eating."

☆ Eat a bite of food and then say, "It is your turn to *eat*" as you sign the word again.

☆ Continue this pattern of eating and feeding as you say and sign the word *eat*.

☆ You can make the sign for *eat* on your child one of two ways:

  ○ Gently place your fingertips on her lips.
  ○ Help her shape the sign by taking her fingers and placing them on her lips.

EAT

3

FOR BABIES 6–9 MONTHS OLD

Physical Development

Babies who are 6–9 months old may

- ☆ Bang objects together
- ☆ Lunge forward or start crawling
- ☆ Sit with little support
- ☆ Get up on all fours and rock
- ☆ Reach accurately for objects
- ☆ Drag objects toward themselves

Social-Emotional Development

Babies who are 6–9 months old may

- ☆ Like to be cuddled and held
- ☆ Jabber and combine syllables
- ☆ Point at objects
- ☆ Want to touch everything
- ☆ Produce a variety of sounds
- ☆ Enjoy nursery rhymes sounds
- ☆ Make two-syllable held sounds
- ☆ Like to look at their reflections in a mirror
- ☆ Enjoy dropping things on purpose
- ☆ Enjoy hearing different volumes and pitches of sounds
- ☆ Enjoy fast and slow rhythms
- ☆ Become aware of body

Intellectual Development

Babies who are 6–9 months old may

- ☆ Learn the names of body parts
- ☆ Analyze what to do with a toy
- ☆ Study objects
- ☆ Understand object permanence

Games and Experiences to Develop Babies' Physical Skills

Bang Together

Developmental milestone: Babies who are 6–9 months old may bang objects together.

☆ Give your baby two wooden spoons or wooden blocks.

☆ Sing one of his favorite songs. As you sing, take his hands and show him how to hit the spoons or blocks to the beat of the song.

☆ This is very good for developing your baby's eye-hand coordination and sense of rhythm.

Rock and Fall

Developmental milestone: Babies who are 6–9 months old may get up on all fours and rock.

☆ Get on all fours on the floor. Encourage your baby to copy you.

☆ Start rocking back and forth and say, "Rocking, rocking, rocking, rocking, then I go boom!" and then fall flat on the floor.

☆ Get back up and repeat.

☆ As your baby copies you, he will strengthen his arm and leg muscles.

☆ Change what you do after you fall on the floor. Some ideas are to turn on your back and kick your legs in the air, turn from side to side, make an animal sound, say "Nighty night," or scoot on your back across the floor.

Touch the Sole

Developmental milestone: Babies who are 6–9 months old may lunge forward or start crawling.

☆ When your child is in a crawling position, gently rub the sole of one foot. He will react to this touch by moving his legs.

☆ Rub the other foot and this will help him learn how to crawl.

Obstacle Course

Developmental milestone: Babies who are 6–9 months old may lunge forward or start crawling.

☆ Help your baby to crawl, creep, and scoot, which develops his coordination.

☆ Make an easy obstacle course by placing soft pillows, blankets, and stuffed animals on the floor. Crawling over these objects strengthens your baby's motor skills.

Crawling All Over

Developmental milestone: Babies who are 6–9 months old may lunge forward or start crawling.

☆ Lie down on the floor and let your baby climb and crawl all over you. Put him on your tummy and let him crawl on or off your tummy.

☆ Put him between your legs and bend your knees so he can wiggle underneath them.

☆ These movements will develop his crawling skills.

Hat Game

Developmental milestone: Babies who are 6–9 months old may reach accurately for objects.

* ☆ This experience develops your baby's vocabulary and eye-hand coordination.
* ☆ Collect several hats that are large enough for your baby to pull off your head.
* ☆ Seat your baby so he is facing you.
* ☆ When you have your baby's attention, put one of the hats on your head and say something your baby will find interesting. This might be something that is funny or that is said with a silly voice. You could say, "Hello, my darling baby! Please take this hat off my head."
* ☆ Bend your head near your baby and let him pull the hat off your head.
* ☆ Put the hat on his head and see if he takes it off of his head.

Roll the Ball

Developmental milestone: Babies who are 6–9 months old may reach accurately for objects.

* ☆ This is a good age to start rolling balls back and forth between you and your baby.
* ☆ Show your baby how to grasp a ball and roll it. (Using a soft fabric ball that has a bell inside makes this game easy and fun.)
* ☆ Sit close to your baby, facing him. Roll the ball to him and encourage him to catch it and then roll it back to you.

☆ As you roll the ball, make this experience more fun by saying words like "Wheee." Praise him when he catches the ball.

☆ This develops your baby's large and fine motor skills.

Fun with Balls

Developmental milestone: Babies who are 6–9 months old may reach accurately for objects.

☆ Balls come in a variety of sizes, shapes, colors, and textures. It is amazing that babies learn that all of these round items are called balls!

☆ Gather a variety of child-safe balls in one basket or box. Dump them out of the basket or box.

☆ Sign *ball* as you hand each ball to your child.

☆ Ask your baby to put the ball in the container.

BALL

☆ Use an animated and playful expression as you hand him each ball and make the sign for the word *ball*.

☆ When all the balls are in the container, dump them out again and repeat the game until your child is ready to stop your ball game.

Sign for *ball*: Bring hands together to form the shape of a ball with curved fingers. Once your baby begins to use the sign (typically at around 9 months to 1 year of age), he may clap or press his palms together.

Back and Forth

Developmental milestone: Babies who are 6–9 months old may sit with little support.

☆ Your baby is getting ready to sit up by himself. This experience will help get him ready for this momentous event and strengthen his back muscles at the same time.

☆ Sit on the floor with your legs spread out. Sit your baby between your legs, facing you with a pillow or cushion propped behind him for balance.

☆ Take his hands and pull him gently forward as you lean back. Then you lean forward and he goes back.

☆ As you do this back-and-forth motion, sing "Row, Row, Row Your Boat."

☆ Once your baby understands what is happening, try doing the movement in rhythm to the song.

Tug a Towel

Developmental milestone: Babies who are 6–9 months old may drag objects toward themselves.

☆ Once your baby can sit up on his own, hold one end of a towel and give him the other end. Gently pull on your end.

☆ Show your baby how to pull his end, and as he does, move your body so that he will think he has pulled you as well. This is great fun for babies and strengthens their arms.

☆ Make comments such as, "You are strong!"

Games and Experiences to Develop Babies' Social-Emotional Skills

I Love You

Developmental milestone: Babies who are 6–9 months old like to be cuddled and held.

☆ Sit in a soft chair and hold your baby in your arms. Gently rock him back and forth as you sing a favorite lullaby or make up words about much you love him.

☆ For example, say, "Baby, baby, (use child's name) I love you. You're so special, you're so special" or say, "Baby, baby, (use child's name) I love you, rocky, rocky, kiss!" and then kiss your child on his forehead.

Nursery Rhymes

Developmental milestone: Babies who are 6–9 months old may make two-syllable sounds.

☆ Nursery rhymes have wonderful words to use to practice two-syllable sounds. Examples include "Peter Piper," "Humpty Dumpty," and "Twinkle, Twinkle, Little Star."

☆ If you know some of these nursery rhymes, you can say them with your baby, otherwise make up your own two-syllable sounds using familiar names that your baby recognizes. For example, "Daddy-waddy," and "doggie-poggie."

☆ Make up a simple story using your words. For example: "One day, daddy-waddy came home to play with baby-waby."

Blow, Blow, Blow

Developmental milestone: Babies who are 6–9 months old may jabber and combine syllables.

☆ When your baby starts to jabber a lot teach him to blow. It will help him learn to control his breath and develop his mouth muscles for speech development.

☆ Show your baby how to purse his lips together and gently blow air out. Blow on his hand and if he likes it, tell him that you are going to blow on his cheek.

☆ See if he can blow on you.

☆ Once he knows how to blow air out try blowing other things, such as a feather or soap bubbles. At this stage, blow the bubbles for your baby. When he gets older, he will be ready to use bubble pipes to blow his own bubbles.

Fill the Day with Words

Developmental milestone: Babies who are 6–9 months old may jabber and combine syllables.

☆ Filling each day with language develops your baby's vocabulary.

☆ When your baby begins to say words such as "more," "up," "bye," "Mama," "dog," or "light," the way you respond to his words makes a difference in his language development.

☆ When your baby says a word, respond with a complete sentence, using that word in the sentence. For example, if your baby says "more," respond with "Would you like some more milk?" Always emphasize the word that your baby used. If your baby says "dog," respond with "That dog has brown fur. It makes a noise that sounds like 'bow wow.'"

Mirror Play

Developmental milestone: Babies who are 6–9 months old may like to look at their reflections in a mirror.

☆ Babies love gazing at themselves in the mirror. Nurture this love by standing or sitting with your baby in front of an unbreakable mirror and making bright, animated facial expressions. Often, your baby will mimic these expressions.

☆ While looking in the mirror with your baby, move in distinctive ways, such as waving your hands, clapping your hands, sticking out your tongue, shaking your head, jumping up and down, or singing a song.

☆ Consider doing these actions and then seeing if your baby repeats what you have done.

Bye, Bye, Light

Developmental milestone: Babies who are 6–9 months old may point at objects.

☆ Let your baby help you turn off the light switch. When the light turns off say, "Bye, bye, light." After a while he'll make the connection between the light being switched off and the room getting dark.

☆ Point to the light and say "light."

☆ Turn off the light and say, "Bye, bye, light," and turn the light off.

Point to the Table

Developmental milestone: Babies who are 6–9 months old may point at objects.

☆ Babies love to point. This is a perfect time to develop their vocabulary and have fun at the same time.

☆ Pick three objects in the room that are familiar to your baby.

☆ As you say each object, take your baby's pointer finger and point toward that object. For example, say "table" and guide your baby's finger to point toward the table.

☆ Continue, selecting other familiar objects to point to.

The Picture Frame Game

Developmental milestone: Babies who are 6–9 months old may point at objects.

☆ On a large piece of cardboard draw the outline of a square picture frame on it. Cut out the square so just the frame remains.

☆ Hold this cardboard frame up to your face so your face is in the cut-out part.

☆ Ask your baby to look at you. Talk to your baby and tell him what you see. Ask him to point to the object that you mention. For example, you would say, "I see baby's nose." He then will point to his nose. If he doesn't, guide his finger to point it to his nose.

☆ Continue doing this with different body parts and objects in the room. Always guide his finger and point if he does not do it himself.

☆ Now let your baby look through the frame. You will have to give him the language, but he will understand and learn many words.

Fill the Basket, Dump It Out

Developmental milestone: Babies who are 6–9 months old may enjoy dropping things on purpose.

☆ Place a large basket or metal pot and several objects in front of your baby.

☆ Place one of the items in the basket or pot. Tell your baby what you are doing.

☆ Encourage your baby to copy you. If he doesn't understand, put one of the objects in his hand and then into the container.

☆ When it drops, say words that indicate that something fell, such as "bumpity bump" or "ding dong."

Watch It Fall

Developmental milestone: Babies who are 6–9 months old may enjoy dropping things on purpose.

☆ Babies like to drop (or throw) things out of their high chair or over the side of the crib. They watch the object fall and listen to the sound it makes when it hits the floor. When your baby does this he is exploring cause-and-effect relationships.

☆ Place your baby in a high chair.

☆ Give him objects that fall and make different sounds, for instance, a rattle, a wooden spoon, a ball, and a washcloth.

☆ Talk about the different sounds. "Oh, that made a soft sound." "That rattle made a big noise!"

Texture Walk

Developmental milestone: Babies who are 6–9 months old may want to touch everything.

☆ Go on a texture walk. Touch different textures and describe how they feel. For example, a pillow is soft, a table top is smooth. The refrigerator is cool and the wall is hard.

☆ Always say the name of what you are touching and then how it feels.

☆ This will build your child's vocabulary.

Sing and Touch

Developmental milestone: Babies who are 6–9 months old may want to touch everything.

☆ This game gives your baby a chance to touch things as he hears the name of the object.

☆ While you hold your baby in your arms, say, "We are going to touch the table, yes, yes, touch the table." Take your baby's hand and put it on the table.

☆ Move to another object and say, "We are going to touch the chair, yes, yes, touch the chair." Take your baby's hand and touch the chair.

☆ Including the words "yes, yes" each time makes the game more fun.

☆ Begin with familiar, everyday objects such as tables, chairs, walls, kitchen items, and so on.

☆ After you have done this a few times with your baby, repeat the names of the same objects and encourage your baby to touch them himself.

I Touch and I Learn

Developmental milestone: Babies who are 6–9 months old may want to touch everything.

☆ Everyone, including babies, learns about objects in the world by touching them, feeling them, and doing things with them. Babies, like the rest of us, need to interact with objects in their world to understand them.

☆ Put a cup, a spoon, and a rattle on a table. Sit with your baby in your lap. First, pick up the cup and pretend to drink from it. Say, "Oh, this is so good."

☆ Now offer the cup to your baby and encourage him to pretend as you did.

☆ Continue with the game, using the spoon and then shaking the rattle.

Bear Voices

Developmental milestone: Babies who are 6–9 months old may enjoy hearing different volumes and pitches of sounds.

☆ This is a wonderful time to read or tell your child the story of "The Three Bears."

☆ After telling your child the story, pretend to be the papa bear and say in a big voice, "I am papa bear. Who has been eating my porridge?"

☆ Repeat with momma and baby bear, changing your voice each time.

Bang on the Drum

Developmental milestone: Babies who are 6–9 months old may enjoy hearing different volumes and pitches of sounds.

☆ Make a large ice-cream carton into a makeshift drum by turning it upside down.

☆ Give your baby two objects of different sizes to use to hit the drum. Suggestions include a large wooden spoon and a small metal spoon.

☆ As your baby uses the two different objects to hit the drum, he will hear a higher and lower sound.

☆ Sing a song that your baby enjoys or clap your hands as he hits the drum.

☆ This game develops your baby's auditory skills.

Different Sounds

Developmental milestone: Babies who are 6–9 months old may enjoy hearing different volumes and pitches of sounds.

☆ Give your baby a wooden spoon.

☆ Encourage him to tap it on different surfaces—on the floor, the table, the chair, the wall, and other surfaces that you select.

☆ You can also prepare surfaces for him to tap—on a plastic container with a lid, a shoebox with a lid, or a paper sack filled with tissue paper.

☆ A good way to play this game is for you to tap first, and then let your baby copy you.

Counting and Popping

Developmental milestone: Babies who are 6–9 months old may enjoy hearing different volumes and pitches of sounds.

- ☆ Babies love an element of surprise.
- ☆ Sit on the floor with your baby. Clap your hands together and say, "Pop."
- ☆ Take your baby's hands, clap them together, and say, "Pop." After you do this a few times, play the following game.
- ☆ Say, "One, two, three, pop." When you say the word *pop*, clap your hands.
- ☆ Repeat this many times, clapping your baby's hands. Vary the speed at which you say the words (and clap your baby's hands) and also the volume, alternating between saying it loudly and softly.
- ☆ Try counting very softly and saying, "Pop" in a big voice
- ☆ Try counting in a big voice and saying, "Pop" in a soft voice.
- ☆ Always clap on the word *pop*.
- ☆ You could also stamp your feet, slap your thigh, and jump on the word *pop*.
- ☆ This is a great language developer, and your baby will learn to listen for the "pop."

Animals Sounds

Developmental milestone: Babies who are 6–9 months old may produce a variety of sounds.

☆ This is a perfect time to introduce animal sounds. "What does the cow say?" "What does the kitty say?"
☆ Look at pictures of animals and make the sounds.
☆ Your baby's language skills will grow and grow.

Hit the Sticks

Developmental milestone: Babies who are 6–9 months old may enjoy fast and slow rhythms.

☆ Sit on the floor with your baby in your lap facing you.
☆ Take two rhythm sticks or wooden spoons. Hold one and give the other to your baby.
☆ Hit the stick on the floor and say, "Boom, boom, boom."
☆ Take your baby's hand with the stick and hit it on the floor and say, "Boom, boom, boom."
☆ This time, tap the stick faster and say the word *boom* faster.
☆ Help your baby do the same thing.
☆ Alternate tapping and saying the word *boom* quickly and slowly.
☆ This experience helps infants begin to understand the concepts of fast and slow.

Recognizing Rhymes

Developmental milestone: Babies who are 6–9 months old may enjoy nursery rhymes.

☆ According to an article in the *Journal of the Acoustical Society of America,* children who enjoy making many sounds will learn to read quicker than others. This means that they learn at an early age to recognize rhymes and the sounds of language.

☆ Saying nursery rhymes, or any rhyme, with infants begins to develop this important language skill.

☆ Make up two sentences that have rhyming words at the end. For example, say, "Give me your hat" and "Give me your cat." Emphasize the ending words *cat* and *hat*.

☆ When babies hear the accented words, they become more aware of their sounds.

Hand and Foot Sounds

Developmental milestone: Babies who are 6–9 months old may become aware of body sounds.

☆ Making sounds with different parts of the body will help your baby become more aware of sounds and names of the parts of his body.

☆ Make each sound and then guide your baby to make the same sound. Hand sounds include clapping your hands, rubbing your hands together, knocking your fists together, and tapping your fingers on the floor. Foot sounds include jumping, stamping, tiptoeing, and marching.

Games and Experiences to Develop Babies' Intellectual/Thinking Skills

Show Me

Developmental milestone: Babies who are 6–9 months old may learn the names of body parts.

✿ Naming your baby's body parts with his name reinforces the learning: "Where is Cindy's nose?" "Here is Cindy's nose." "Where are Cindy's fingers?" "Here are Cindy's fingers."

✿ Soon your baby will show you the parts that you are naming.

Ten Fingers

Developmental milestone: Babies who are 6–9 months old may learn the names of body parts.

✿ One of the first things a baby discovers is his hands. He puts them in his mouth, grasps them together, and uses them to hold things.

✿ Here is a game to teach your baby about the parts of his body and have fun at the same time.

✿ Sit your baby near you.

✿ Take off his shoes and socks and say and do the following.

✿ Say, "Here are baby's fingers. Put them on your head," as you put his fingers on his head.

✿ Say, "Here are baby's fingers. Put them on your toes," as you put his fingers on his toes.

✿ Say, "Here are baby's fingers. Put them on your ears," as you put his fingers on his ears.

✿ Continue with different parts of the body.

Diaper Game

Developmental milestone: Babies who are 6–9 months old may learn the names of body parts.

☆ A good game to play during diaper-changing time is one in which you name body parts with singing. Infants enjoy hearing music and the melodies attract their attention.

☆ Pick one of your favorite songs or make up a melody of your own.

☆ Sing about your baby's body parts as you lovingly touch each one. Start by naming his feet and move up to the tummy, the elbows, the shoulders, and, finally, his face.

Hold the Toy

Developmental milestone: Babies who are 6–9 months old may analyze what to do with a toy.

☆ Give your baby two small toys, one for each hand.

☆ While he is holding the toys, offer him a third toy and help him figure out how to put one toy down in order to pick up the next one.

☆ Hand him a toy and say, "One for you." Now say, "One for me" as you take a toy.

☆ Repeat "One for you" as you hand him another toy. Repeat "One for me" as you take another toy.

☆ Say, "One for you" and encourage him to put down one of the two toys he is holding to take the next one.

Move the Ball

Developmental milestone: Babies who are 6–9 months old may analyze what to do with a toy.

☆ Give your baby a small rubber ball to hold in his hands. Let him experiment with rolling the ball and playing with it in any other way.
☆ Take the ball and place it in a large zipper-closure bag. The bag should be large enough for the ball to move around inside.
☆ Let your baby experiment with pushing the ball around in the bag, stopping it and moving it in many directions.
☆ This is great fun for your baby and develops his eye-hand coordination.
   Safety note: Do not let your baby do this unsupervised. Also, put away the plastic bag when the game is over.

Something Different

Developmental milestone: Babies who are 6–9 months old may study objects.

☆ Find two pictures in a magazine that are exactly the same or draw two simple pictures that are exactly the same.
☆ Show these two pictures to your baby and name some of the items in the pictures. For example, say, "Look at the boy" while pointing to the boy in one picture, repeat the words, and then point to the boy in the second picture.
☆ After you have looked at the pictures for a while, add something, such as a ball, tree, or zigzag line, to one of the pictures.

☆ Show your baby the new item on one of the pictures. Then show the second picture and ask, "Where is the [new item]?"

☆ If your baby is not ready to find a new item on the second picture, add it to the picture while your baby is watching.

☆ This kind of activity sets the stage for recognizing letters and reading experiences in the future.

Find the Toy

Developmental milestone: Babies who are 6–9 months old may understand object permanence.

☆ Hold up one of your baby's favorite toys. Say its name and put it down.

☆ Hold it up again and say, "I am putting it behind me." Be sure your baby is watching you as you put the toy behind you.

☆ Ask your baby, "Where is the [name of toy]?" If he knows the answer (by pointing to you or moving to where the toy is), praise him enthusiastically.

☆ Play this again, but this time put the toy behind your baby's back and see if he can figure out where it is.

☆ The final developmental stage of this game is for your baby to put the toy behind his back himself. When he can do this, he understands the concept.

4 FOR BABIES 9–12 MONTHS OLD

Physical Development

Babies who are 9–12 months old may

☆ Master crawling with their tummy off the ground
☆ Wiggle, kick, and shake their legs
☆ Enjoy putting objects into containers
☆ Pick things up using a pincer grasp
☆ Have good hand and finger coordination
☆ Transfer objects from one hand to the other, and then back
☆ Enjoy feeling different textures
☆ Like to roll balls
☆ Clap their hands or wave bye-bye, if prompted
☆ Walk with help

Social-Emotional Development

Babies who are 9–12 months old may

☆ Say "no" and shake their head
☆ Like to look at books with you
☆ Copy and imitate your actions
☆ Like to sing
☆ Laugh at funny things
☆ Say several words

Intellectual Development

Babies who are 9–12 months old may

☆ Say "Mama" and "Dada" to the correct person
☆ Understand the meaning of words in context
☆ Follow simple directions
☆ Recognize pictures in books or magazines
☆ Begin to understand cause and effect
☆ Understand the meaning of words they hear
☆ Like to pretend
☆ Understand the signs that they have learned
☆ Respond to familiar questions with actions or words

Games and Experiences to Develop Babies' Physical Skills

Crawl Across

Developmental milestone: Babies who are 9–12 months old may master crawling with their tummy off the ground.

* ☆ Crawling encourages cross patterning activities and develops brain pathways for walking.
* ☆ Add to your baby's experience of crawling by standing with your legs apart and letting her crawl through your legs.
* ☆ Additionally, try lying down on the floor and letting her crawl over your back.
* ☆ Alternate these two experiences for crawling.

Under Your Legs

Developmental milestone: Babies who are 9–12 months old may master crawling with their tummy off the ground.

* ☆ Sit on the floor and prop your legs up together with knees bent. Make room so that your baby can crawl under your legs.
* ☆ Put one of your child's toys under your legs so that she has to crawl under your legs to retrieve the toy.
* ☆ When your baby is directly under your legs, open them and say, "Peek-a-boo." She will absolutely love this!
* ☆ Repeat until your baby tires of the experience.

Make a Tunnel

Developmental milestone: Babies who are 9–12 months old may master crawling with their tummy off the ground.

☆ Use several boxes to make a tunnel.

☆ Sit at one end of the tunnel, look through it, and call to your baby.

☆ Encourage your baby to crawl through the tunnel to reach you. If she does not understand, crawl through the tunnel to show her how to do it.

☆ This is a very good game for developing the skill of perception.

Wiggle Around

Developmental milestone: Babies who are 9–12 months old may wiggle, kick, and shake their legs.

☆ Give babies the freedom to move around. Young infants enjoy being on their backs so that they can kick, wiggle, and look around.

☆ Lie down on your back with your baby beside you.

☆ Wiggle and shake your legs and encourage her to copy you.

☆ Roll from side to side and help her do the same motions.

In and Out

Developmental milestone: Babies who are 9–12 months old may enjoy putting objects into containers.

☆ Explore how much your baby enjoys taking her toys out of a container.

☆ Choose three objects, such as a ball, a spoon, and a car, and put them into a small box.

☆ As you put each object in the box, say its name.

☆ Ask your baby to take out the spoon. When she does, give her lots of praise.

Colorful Scarves

Developmental milestone: Babies who are 9–12 months old may enjoy putting objects into containers.

☆ Tie several colorful scarves or pieces of fabric together. Insert one end into a cardboard tube and let your baby pull them out.

☆ Push the scarves into the cardboard tube again as you show your baby how to play the game. Let your baby help you push the scarves into the tube.

☆ As you pull the scarves out, talk about the pretty colors and the silky, smooth textures.

☆ Offer your baby the scarves and encourage her to put them into the tube.

Exploring Outside

Developmental milestone: Babies who are 9–12 months old may enjoy putting objects into containers.

☆ Exploring the world outdoors is something your baby will enjoy.
☆ Take a basket outside and place objects that you find in the basket. Look for leaves, twigs, blades of grass, and wildflowers.
☆ Talking about the items with your little one will develop her vocabulary.

Nesting Cups

Developmental milestone: Babies who are 9–12 months old may enjoy putting objects into containers.

☆ While your baby watches, nest several different-sized plastic cups.
☆ Give your baby the largest cup, followed by the next size, and so on.
☆ Encourage her to put each cup that you give her inside the previous cup.
☆ When you are finished, clap your hands, and shout, "Hooray!" to celebrate.
☆ Separate the cups and let your baby play with them as you watch and help when necessary. Each time your baby nests one cup inside another, clap your hands and shout, "Hooray!"

Zipper!

Developmental milestone: Babies who are 9–12 months old may pick things up using a pincer grasp.

☆ Show your baby a zipper on a piece of clothing and then show her how to move the zipper up and down.

☆ This is a great way to practice the fine motor development needed for a pincer grip (to hold things between the thumb and forefinger).

☆ Say, "One, two, threeeeeeee, zip." When you say, "Zip," move the zipper.

Stick the Toy

Developmental milestone: Babies who are 9–12 months old may pick things up using a pincer grasp.

☆ When your baby has mastered the ability to pick up and manipulate toys, try this fun experience that will develop her fine motor skills and eye-hand coordination.

☆ Remove the backing from a piece of contact paper. Place it on the floor, sticky side up. Tape it down securely on all four sides.

☆ Gather an assortment of small toys and stick them on the paper.

☆ Show your baby the toys and encourage her to pick them up.

☆ It is great fun to unstick the toys. Your baby will also want to stick them back on the paper.

☆ Show her how to stick her finger on the paper.

Open, Close

Developmental milestone: Babies who are 9–12 months old may have good hand and finger coordination.

- ☆ Your baby needs to learn to use her hands to do many things, including playing with toys and feeding and dressing herself.
- ☆ Show your baby how to open and close her hands. Following are some ways to practice this skill.
- ☆ Say the following actions and do them with your baby. Do the same actions with each hand separately.
  - ○ Close your fingers.
  - ○ Open your fingers.
  - ○ Shake your fingers.
  - ○ Close your fingers.
  - ○ Open your fingers.
  - ○ Shake your fingers.
- ☆ Repeat the actions with your hands high in the air.

Turn, Turn

Developmental milestone: Babies who are 9–12 months old may have good hand and finger coordination.

- ☆ Being able to turn one's wrists is an important fine motor skill that needs to be practiced.
- ☆ Take your baby's wrist as you say "wrist." Show her how to move her wrist around and up and down.
- ☆ While you are holding her hand, gently move her wrist up, down, and around.
- ☆ Repeat this several times and then encourage her to do it by herself as she watches you move your wrist up, down, and around.

Lids Off!

Developmental milestone: Babies who are 9–12 months old may have good hand and finger coordination.

- ☆ Babies need to problem solve through free exploration. This game will give them that opportunity.
- ☆ Find three objects with lids that are easy to put on and take off. For example, a cooking pot, a shoebox, and a plastic container.
- ☆ Put the lid on each item as your baby watches.
- ☆ Take off the lids and then ask your baby to put the lid back on.
- ☆ Help your baby only if she asks for it. You will be fascinated as you watch your baby's young mind figure out what to do.

Hand to Hand

Developmental milestone: Babies who are 9–12 months old may transfer objects from one hand to the other, and then back.

- ☆ Give your baby two paper cups and a piece of dry cereal.
- ☆ Show your baby how to pour the cereal from one cup to the other.
- ☆ Your baby will delight in playing this game, which develops her fine motor skills.

Sights and Smells

Developmental milestone: Babies who are 9–12 months old may enjoy feeling different textures.

☆ Every time your baby uses one of her senses, a connection, or path, is made in her brain.
Note: Although this experience uses a pumpkin, you can use many different materials from other fruits and vegetables to a cardboard box.

☆ Go to the supermarket and buy a small pumpkin. Talk about the pumpkin and look at pictures of pumpkins in magazines.

☆ Open up the top of the pumpkin and look inside with your baby.

☆ Smell the pumpkin and feel the insides. Feel the seeds and squishy pulp.

☆ As you help your infant explore the inside of the pumpkin, describe the experience: "Oh, it smells so good." "Oh, it feels slimy."

Here Comes the Ball

Developmental milestone: Babies who are 9–12 months old may like to roll balls.

☆ Sit on the floor opposite your baby.

☆ Roll the ball to her and encourage her to roll it back.

☆ When you roll the ball, say, "One, two, three, here comes the ball." Say, "One, two" softly and say, "Three" in a louder, excited voice.

☆ Soon your baby will be waiting for you to say "three" so that she can roll the ball.

☆ This game develops your baby's motor skills and listening skills and begins to teach her how to take turns.

Push the Stroller

Developmental milestone: Babies who are 9–12 months old may walk with help.

- ☆ Let your baby practice walking while holding onto a stroller. Help your child push the stroller and then stop.
- ☆ Push again and then stop.
- ☆ As you push and stop say, "I walk, walk, walk, and then I stop."
- ☆ Repeat several times.
- ☆ Your baby will enjoy this, and she will be practicing walking at the same time.

Textures on My Feet

Developmental milestone: Babies who are 9–12 months old may walk with help.

- ☆ Walking with bare feet on different textures helps your baby develop her balance, and it also is a good sensory experience.
- ☆ Place different materials on the floor that will provide different touch sensations. Suggestions include carpet squares; large, flat sponges; linoleum squares; and pillows.
- ☆ Hold your child's hands as she walks on the different textures. Describe how each texture might feel to your baby. "This feels smooth" or "This feels soft" are some things you might say.
- ☆ This game also develops your baby's balance and language skills.

One, Two, Three, Clap

Developmental milestone: Babies who are 9–12 months old may clap their hands or wave "bye-bye," if prompted.

☆ Playing this game is also an introduction to counting.

☆ Count, "One, two" in a very soft voice. Say, "Three" louder and clap your hands.

☆ You can add movements to the clap, such as clap and jump up and down, turn around, bend at the waist, and so on.

☆ Your baby will love trying to copy you.

Games and Experiences to Develop Babies' Social-Emotional Skills

No!

Developmental milestone: Babies who are 9–12 months old may say "no" and shake their heads.

- ☆ Chant the following words twice; shake your head "no" each time you say "no." "No, no, no, I like to say 'no.'"
- ☆ Say, "No, no, no, no, no, no, no, no, no, no. I like to say 'no.'"
- ☆ Repeat, substituting "no" for "yes." Be sure to shake your head up and down each time you say "yes."

Look at the Picture

Developmental milestone: Babies who are 9–12 months old may like to look at books with you.

- ☆ Cut out colorful pictures from magazines and paste them into a blank notebook.
- ☆ Select familiar pictures like those of a telephone, a dog, a car, a carrot, or a ball.
- ☆ Sit with your baby and look at the pictures together. As you look at them, talk about each picture. For example, say, "This is a picture of a telephone. Where is the telephone?"

Looking at Books

Developmental milestone: Babies who are 9–12 months old may like to look at books with you.

☆ Looking at books together encourages your baby's language development. It is important at this young age to let your baby be the guide. She might be willing to look at books for only a very short time.

☆ The following is a way that might keep her looking at books longer. Start with an animal book and ask, "Where is the cow?" As you ask, put your finger on the picture of the cow as you say "cow." Ask the same question again and put her finger on the cow as you say "cow."

☆ Continue with other animals and with books that focus on other topics.

A Family Book

Developmental milestone: Babies who are 9–12 months old may like to look at books with you.

☆ Make a family book to read with your child by creating a book with a photo of one family member on each page.

☆ As you read the book with your child, comment on the details of the picture. For example, "Grandma is wearing a red dress" or "Aunt Mary has a pretty smile."

☆ Remember to include pictures of family pets.

☆ This develops your baby's language skills and teaches her how to turn pages in a book, and it is also a lovely bonding experience for you and your baby.

Filling in the Blanks

Developmental milestone: Babies who are 9–12 months old may like to look at books with you.

☆ Reading to your baby regularly will greatly increase her vocabulary development.

☆ When reading a book to your baby, get her attention by pointing to a picture and saying, "Look, there's a kitty!" If your baby points or responds verbally, be sure to respond. For example, you could say, "Yes, the kitty is climbing a tree."

☆ What you are doing is filling in the words for what your baby cannot say. This kind of dialogue is intellectually stimulating for your baby.

☆ The ultimate reward is a bigger vocabulary for your baby.

Can You Copy Me?

Developmental milestone: Babies who are 9–12 months old may copy and imitate your actions.

☆ Play "follow the leader" with your baby. She will enjoy trying to imitate you. Some of the things you can do are the following:
  ○ Wiggle your fingers as you say, "Wiggle, wiggle, wiggle."
  ○ Open and close your fist.
  ○ Stick out your tongue.
  ○ Make the raspberry sound with your mouth.
  ○ Blow air.

Sounds Like

Developmental milestone: Babies who are 9–12 months old may copy and imitate your actions.

☆ Show your baby how she can make all kinds of sounds with her mouth.

☆ Sit your baby in a place where she can see your face clearly.

☆ Make noises with your mouth and encourage her to copy you. Ideas include making kissing sounds, popping your lips, blowing your lips like a motorboat, growling, squealing, gurgling, cooing, humming, and making animal sounds.

Comb Your Hair

Developmental milestone: Babies who are 9–12 months old may copy and imitate your actions.

☆ This wonderful game develops your baby's fine motor skills.

☆ Sit on the floor with your baby. Comb your hair as she watches. Say, "I am combing my hair."

☆ Comb your baby's hair. Say, "I am combing [your child's name] hair."

☆ Take a doll with hair and comb the doll's hair. Say, "I am combing the doll's hair."

☆ Give the comb to your baby. Hold the doll and say, "[your child's name], can you comb the doll's hair?"

☆ Guide her hand if necessary.

Do You Want More?

Developmental milestone: Babies who are 9–12 months old may copy and imitate your actions.

MORE

* *More* is a perfect sign to help your baby understand the power of words. There are many opportunities for you to ask your child, "Do you want more?" and show him the sign for *more:*
  * As you feed her or offer her a drink
  * While you sing, rock, or snuggle at bedtime
  * When you are playing or dancing
* If she vocalizes or attempts to sign, tell her, "Thank you for telling me *more*," and then give her what she desires, such as more food or drink, or to rock or play.
* You can also take her fingers and gently shape the *more* sign with her hands. Then tell her, "Good signing *more*" and offer her what she requested!

Shake That Rattle!

Developmental milestone: Babies who are 9–12 months old may like to sing.

* Give your baby a rattle so they begin to understand that they can participate in the world of music and sound.
* Sing familiar songs and encourage your baby to shake the rattle.
* When your baby is ready, give her wooden spoons and pots and pans to tap as you sing along.

Sing This Song!

Developmental milestone: Babies who are 9–12 months old may like to sing.

☆ Select three or four of your child's favorite songs. Find toys or other objects that illustrate words in the songs, for example, a picture of a spider for "Eensy Weensy Spider" or a toy cow for "Old MacDonald Had a Farm."

☆ Put the objects into a bag or box.

☆ Give the box to your baby and let her take an object out of the bag and then sing the song that goes with the object.

☆ You can have more than one object to represent a song. For example, place a toy mouse and a clock in the bag or box for "Hickory, Dickory, Dock."

☆ This is a great way to develop your baby's language skills.

Say the Name

Developmental milestone: Babies who are 9–12 months old may say several words.

☆ Sit on the floor with your baby.

☆ Take two of her favorite toys and put them in front of you.

☆ Pick up the first toy (for example, a ball) and say, "This is a ball." Pick up the second toy (for example, a car) and say, "This is a car."

☆ Pick up the first toy again and say, "This is a ..." Leave out the word and see if your baby can say the name of the toy.

☆ Keep adding words as she gets better at the game. This is a wonderful way to develop your baby's vocabulary.

Hello!

Developmental milestone: Babies who are 9–12 months old may say several words.

☆ Pick up a pretend phone and talk into it using words that your baby knows.

☆ Say things such as "Hello, [child's name], I love you."

☆ Your baby might enjoy hearing you sing a song into the phone.

☆ Give the phone to your baby so she can talk on the phone.

Toy Conversations

Developmental milestone: Babies who are 9–12 months old may say several words.

☆ Using your baby's toys as puppets that are having a conversation is a wonderful way to develop your baby's language skills.

☆ Choose a toy, such as a toy car, for yourself, and give your baby a stuffed animal.

☆ The following is a conversation that could take place between the stuffed animal and the car. You will do all the speaking, for the car and for the stuffed animal.

You: "I'm a car. I can take you for a ride."

Baby: "I like the car." (Help your baby move the stuffed animal up and down as if it is talking.)

You: "We could go on a trip to the park in a car."

Baby: "The park is fun. I can see the squirrels."

☆ Continue this conversation as you encourage your baby to respond with words, smiles, actions, and so on.

☆ This is an enjoyable way to increase your baby's vocabulary.

Where Is the Spoon?

Developmental milestone: Babies who are 9–12 months old may say several words.

✭ This experience builds your baby's vocabulary skills. The repetition also develops memory skills.

✭ Pick up an object or a toy. For example, pick up a spoon and say, "This is a spoon, a very shiny spoon."

✭ Hide the spoon behind your back and say, "Where is the spoon, the very shiny spoon?"

✭ Bring the spoon out from behind your back and say, "Here is the spoon, the very shiny spoon."

✭ Each time you say, "Here is the spoon," put your baby's hand on the spoon.

✭ Repeat with other objects. Start with objects that are familiar to your baby.

Funny Things

Developmental milestone: Babies who are 9–12 months old may laugh at funny things.

✭ Because your baby is developing a sense of humor, do funny things to make her laugh:

  ○ Pretend to drink from her bottle or sippy cup.
  ○ Pretend to put on some of her clothes or shoes.

Laugh Your Stress Away

Developmental milestone: Babies who are 9–12 months old may laugh at funny things.

☆ Laughter reduces stress and creates a relaxing atmosphere.

☆ Puff up your cheeks and tell your baby to touch your nose. When she does, let the air out of your cheeks. Encourage her to try it.

☆ Pull your ear and stick out your tongue. Ask your baby to pull your ear and when she does, stick your tongue out.

☆ Ask your baby to pat your head. When she does, make a funny sound.

☆ These are great fun for you and your baby. Be ready to do these activities over and over!

Games and Experiences to Develop Babies' Intellectual/Thinking Skills

Family Pictures

Developmental milestone: Babies who are 9–12 months old may say "Mama" and "Dada" to the correct person.

★ Gather together several pictures of family and friends.
★ Say to your baby, "I wonder how dada is today. Let's find his picture."
★ Show your baby two or three pictures, one of which is of her father. Help your child identify her daddy.
★ Repeat with other family members.
★ This experience develops your baby's sense of belonging.

Bouncy, Bouncy

Developmental milestone: Babies who are 9–12 months old may understand the meaning of words in context.

★ Enjoy this bouncy game with your baby: Sit on a chair with your child on your knees. She should be facing you. Hold her at her waist.
★ Say, "Bouncy, bouncy, up" as you bounce your child and hold her up in the air.
★ Say, "Bouncy, bouncy, down," as you open your knees and let her bottom drop through your open knees.
★ Say, "Bouncy, bouncy, in" as you bring your baby toward you.
★ Say, "Bouncy, bouncy, out" as you move her away from you.
★ Finally, say "up, down, in, and out" and do each action as you say the word.

The Tree

Developmental milestone: Babies who are 9–12 months old may understand the meaning of words in context.

- ☆ Choose a word and use it in many different ways with your baby. For example, if you choose the word "tree," you can do the following:
    - ○ Go outside and touch a tree as you say "tree."
    - ○ Use the word tree in a sentence.
    - ○ Sit under a tree.
    - ○ Notice that the tree is tall.
    - ○ Look at the beautiful leaves that the tree has.
- ☆ Make up songs or poems that use the word "tree."
- ☆ Do this for several days and then when you are outside, ask your baby, "Where is the tree?"

Repeat the Words

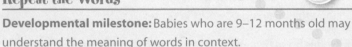

Developmental milestone: Babies who are 9–12 months old may understand the meaning of words in context.

- ☆ According to Linda Acredolo and Susan Goodwyn in *Baby Minds*, babies whose parents and caretakers speak to them extensively have significantly higher IQs and more extensive vocabularies when they get older than other children, so interaction is especially important right now.
- ☆ Use a variety of words when you talk to your baby by describing your surroundings on a walk, at the supermarket, and in the car.

☆ Repeat some of the same words you used later in the day. For example, if you saw apples at the supermarket, say, "We saw apples and oranges at the supermarket today," or if you went to the park, say, "We saw many children at the park."

☆ Repeating familiar words will build your baby's vocabulary.

One

Developmental milestone: Babies who are 9–12 months old may understand the meaning of words in context.

☆ According to www.smartbaby.com, studies suggest that babies begin to understand the concept of one at an early age. The following is a game that researchers use to show that infants understand this concept.

☆ When you have your baby's attention, point your right index finger upward and say, "One."

☆ Bring your right index finger down to form a fist again and point your right fifth finger up and say, "One." Pause for several seconds, and say, "One" again.

☆ Bring down the fifth finger to form a fist again.

☆ Point your right thumb up and say, "One." Pause for several seconds and say "One" again.

☆ You have demonstrated the concept of "one" three times using your index finger, fifth finger, and thumb.

☆ Repeat the same method with your other hand.

Teddy Bear's Nose

Developmental milestone: Babies who are 9–12 months old may understand the meaning of words in context.

☆ This game of naming body parts will build your baby's vocabulary and develop her cognitive thinking.

☆ You will need a stuffed animal or teddy bear to play the game.

☆ Touch your nose and say, "This is my nose."

☆ Touch your baby's nose and say, "This is your nose."

☆ Touch the stuffed animal's nose and say, "This is teddy's nose."

☆ Ask your baby to touch your nose, her nose, and teddy's nose.

☆ Repeat the game, using other parts of the body.

Shake, Baby, Shake

Developmental milestone: Babies who are 9–12 months old may follow simple directions.

☆ Place a rattle in your hand and give another rattle to your baby.

☆ Shake your rattle and say to your baby, "Shake the rattle."

☆ Take your baby's hand with the rattle and shake it. As you shake the rattle, say "Shake the rattle."

☆ Do this several times so that your baby hears the words that you say.

☆ Say, "Shake the rattle" to your baby and see if she responds by shaking her rattle.

☆ This experience enhances your child's listening skills.

Right Side Up

Developmental milestone: Babies who are 9–12 months old may follow simple directions.

☆ Turn two of your baby's favorite toys upside down.

☆ Ask her to turn them right side up. You may have to show her how to do this.

☆ When she is successful, praise her enthusiastically.

☆ This activity develops your child's thinking skills.

Simple Things Are Best

Developmental milestone: Babies who are 9–12 months old may follow simple directions.

☆ Ask your baby to do simple things, such as the following:

  ○ Wave "bye-bye."

  ○ Clap her hands together.

  ○ Touch her nose.

  ○ Throw a kiss.

  ○ Make a sound like a cow.

☆ This experience develops your child's listening skills and helps you understand what she does and does not understand.

☆ If you find that she cannot follow some of the directions, change them to a simpler action so she is successful. When your baby is ready, ask her to do more complex actions.

Wipe Your Face

Developmental milestone: Babies who are 9–12 months old may follow simple directions.

☆ Encouraging your baby's independence by developing her self-help skills builds her self-confidence and self-esteem.

☆ After she finishes eating, give her a warm cloth and let her wipe her face and hands. Show her how to wipe each finger individually as you say "one finger clean, hip, hip, hooray." Repeat for each finger.

☆ This develops your child's fine motor skills.

Under the Blanket

Developmental milestone: Babies who are 9–12 months old may follow simple directions.

☆ This game develops your baby's observation skills and demonstrates the concept of "under."

☆ Let your baby watch as you hide a small toy or book under a pillow.

☆ After you hide the toy or book, ask her to find it.

☆ If she does not understand, ask her again and then take her to the pillow and show her that the toy or book is under the pillow.

☆ Tell her that you are going to hide the toy or book under a blanket and then ask her to get the toy or book from under the blanket.

☆ Keep hiding the toy or book different places that are "under" something.

Pictures, Pictures

Developmental milestone: Babies who are 9–12 months old may recognize pictures in books or magazines.

* Cut out a magazine picture that is familiar to your baby. Animals are good to start with.
* Talk with your baby about the picture, pointing out the face, the tail, the ears, and other features.
* Cut the picture into two pieces (an adult-only step).
* Help your baby put the two parts together so that the animal's tail and head are in the right place.
* This is great fun for your baby as she learns memory and concentration skills.
* Cut two pictures in half and mix them up. Help your baby match the correct halves.

On and Off, Open and Close

Developmental milestone: Babies who are 9–12 months old may begin to understand cause and effect.

* Babies at this age are learning that they can make things happen. By pulling on a knob, they can open a cupboard door. They love to turn on light switches, television remotes, and dishwashers.
* Describe what is happening so your baby begins to understand that she can make certain things happen by pushing a button, opening a door, or flipping a switch.
* Add to your baby's cause-and-effect experiences by helping her roll a ball into a tower of blocks. Say, "You knocked down the blocks!"

Describe the Action

Developmental milestone: Babies who are 9–12 months old may understand the meaning of words they hear.

☆ Describe your baby's actions: "Timmy, you picked up the block and put it down" or "Laura, look at your pretty shoes! You took them off your feet."

☆ The more words your baby hears, the more language she will have and the better reader she will be. (For more information, visit the website of the International Reading Association— www.reading.org.)

☆ You are the person who can teach your baby a love of language.

Name the Toy

Developmental milestone: Babies who are 9–12 months old may understand the meaning of words they hear.

☆ Place a few familiar toys into a shoebox. Some ideas are a cup, a toy car, a spoon, a block, and a book.

☆ Take each item out of the box and say its name.

☆ When all the items are out of the box, put them back in the box.

☆ Ask your baby to give you one of the items. When she gives it to you, say, "Thank you for giving me the [name of item]."

☆ The more you play naming games with your baby, the better language skills she will have.

Faces

Developmental milestone: Babies who are 9–12 months old may understand the meaning of words they hear.

☆ This game develops your baby's cognitive thinking and helps her learn to identify parts of the face.

☆ Cut out a picture of a face from a magazine.

☆ Show your baby the face. Touch and name the eyes, nose, and mouth.

☆ Touch and name your baby's eyes, nose, and mouth.

☆ Repeat with your eyes, nose, and mouth.

☆ Do this a few times and then ask your baby where the nose is. She may touch her nose, your nose, or the picture's nose. All are correct.

Pretend to Sip

Developmental milestone: Babies who are 9–12 months old may like to pretend.

☆ When your baby is learning to drink from a cup, sit next to the baby and place a stuffed animal sitting next to you.

☆ To encourage your baby to drink from the cup, give the stuffed animal a pretend sip of the drink and then give your baby a sip.

☆ This also develops your baby's creativity.

Time for Soup

Developmental milestone: Babies who are 9–12 months old may like to pretend.

☆ Give your baby a plastic bowl and tell her that you are going to make some soup.

☆ Name vegetables that are familiar to your baby, such as carrots, potatoes, and green beans, and pretend to put them into the soup.

☆ Give your child a spoon to stir the soup. When it is "cooked," pretend to eat the soup using the spoon.

☆ This creative experience develops your baby's fine motor skills.

Butterflies

Developmental milestone: Babies who are 9–12 months old may like to pretend.

☆ This is a wonderful example of how children learn through play. **Note:** The game will be more meaningful if you look at pictures of butterflies with your baby before you do the activity.

☆ Sit on the floor and hold your baby in your lap with her back facing you.

☆ Have her curl up like a ball (use the word "cocoon" if it is familiar) and curl your body over hers.

☆ As you say, "Butterfly, butterfly, where are you?" in a sing-song voice, slowly unfold your body and your baby's body.

☆ Lift her in the air and tell her to move her arms like wings.

☆ When you lift her in the air, say, "Beautiful, beautiful butterfly, there you are!" in a sing-song voice.

Let Me Help You

Developmental milestone: Babies who are 9–12 months old may understand the signs that they have learned.

☆ Babies this age have a list of things they want and need, and usually the only way they can ask for them is by crying or fussing.

EAT

☆ Give your baby's wishes a label and respond to them: "You must be hungry and want a snack so let's go eat," or "You want to take a stroller ride outside, so we will take one after we change your diaper." It's never too early for a child to learn that caring and attentive adults can respond to a child's "I want!"

PLAY

☆ Your child may continue to fuss if you have not correctly guessed what is troubling her. Persist in playing this "problem-solving game" with your child, signing and saying the words your child is unable to tell you with her voice, such as *eat, play, milk,* or *bed*. When she is ready, she may use those signs to tell you what she wants and needs.

MILK

BED/SLEEP

So Big!

Developmental milestone: Babies who are 9–12 months old may respond to familiar questions with actions or words.

The popular game of "So Big!" encourages your baby to express herself.

☆ Ask your baby, "How big are you?" If she does not raise her arms, gently lift her hands high over her head and say, "So big!"

☆ After doing this several times, your baby will lift her arms on her own when you say, "So big!"

Watch Me Sign

Developmental milestone: Babies who are 9–12 months old may respond to familiar questions with actions or words.

☆ Babies at this age are beginning to understand language; they are figuring out that your spoken and signed words mean something.

☆ They respond to your words and gestures by looking, smiling, touching, or pointing when you ask questions such as, "Where is daddy?" or say, "Point to the doggie on this page of the book."

☆ Your baby will begin to respond to your words by following simple directions, such as "Please eat the cereal on your high chair tray" or "Give me a big hug!"

☆ Help your baby master the connection between your spoken and signed words by always signing as you speak a few key vocabulary words, such as the signs shared in this book.

☆ Be consistent with your signing and give your baby plenty of opportunities to observe and practice. Repetition is essential for her to learn to communicate with sign language. Continue to use your hands on top of hers so that she can feel the signs with her own fingers.

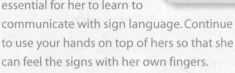

PLAY   MORE

Give Me the Toy

Developmental milestone: Babies who are 9–12 months old may respond to familiar questions with actions or words.

DOG

☆ Play a "language understanding" game. Place two or three of your baby's favorite toys on the floor, such as a ball and toy dog.
☆ Ask her to touch or hand you the ball. Then repeat for the dog. Sign the words *dog* and *ball* as you speak them.

BALL

☆ Respond with smiles, hugs, and a thank you for "giving me the ball!"
☆ You can play the same game with pictures in a picture book. Ask your child to point to the ball or dog on the page in the book.

Sign for *dog*: Pat leg with closed hand as if calling a dog. Once your baby begins to use the sign (typically at around 9 months to 1 year of age), she may pat one or both legs.

Sign for *ball*: Bring hands together to form the shape of a ball with curved fingers. Once your baby begins to use the sign (typically at around 9 months to 1 year of age), she may clap or press her palms together.

REFERENCES AND RESOURCES

Books

Acredolo, L., & Goodwyn, S. (2000). *Baby minds: Brain-building games your baby will love.* New York: Bantam Books.

Barnet, A., & Barnet, R. (1998). *The youngest minds: Parenting and genes in the development of intellect and emotion.* New York: Simon and Schuster.

Bergen, D., Reid, R., & Torelli, L. (2001). *Educating and caring for very young children: The infant/toddler curriculum.* New York: Teachers College Press.

Berk, L. (2000). *Child development (5th ed.).* Needham Heights, MA: Allyn & Bacon.

Charner, K., Murphy, M., & Clark C. (Eds.). (2006). *The encyclopedia of infant and toddler activities.* Beltsville, MD: Gryphon House.

Crowe, R., & Connell, G. (2004). *Moving to learn.* Christchurch, New Zealand: Caxton Press.

Hirsh-Pasek, K., & Golinkoff, R. M. (2003). *Einstein never used flash cards: How our children really learn—and why they need to play more and memorize less.* New York: Rodale.

Hoff-Ginsberg, E. (1997). *Language development.* Pacific Grove, CA: Brooks/Cole.

Oberlander, J. (2007). *Fun start.* London: Harper Thorson.

Oesterreich, L. (1995). *Ages & stages: Newborn to 1 year.* In L. Oesterreich, B. Holt, & S. Karas, S. Iowa family child care handbook. Ames, IA: Iowa State University Extension.

Silberg, J. (1999). *125 brain games for babies.* Beltsville, MD: Gryphon House.

Silberg, J. (2001). *Games to play with babies (3rd ed.).* Beltsville, MD: Gryphon House.

Articles

Arnold, R., & Colburn, N. (2005). Oh! What a smart baby—What you need to know about children's brain development. *School Library Journal,* 51(2), 37.

Brannon, E. M. (2002, April). The development of ordinal numerical knowledge in infancy. *Cognition,* 83, 223–240.

DeNoon, D. J. (2007, August 7). "Smart baby" DVDs no help, may harm. *WebMD Medical News.* Available online at children.webmd.com/news/ 20070807/smart-baby-dvds-no-help-may-harm.

Gopnik, A. (1996). The Post-Piaget era. *Psychological Science.* 7 (4), 221–225.

Kuhl, P. K., & Meltzoff, A. N. (1996). Infant vocalizations in response to speech: Vocal imitation and developmental change. *Journal of the Acoustical Society of America,* 100(4), 2425–2438.

McGaha, C. (2003). The importance of the senses for infants. *Focus on Infants and Toddlers* 16 (1).

Nitschke, J. B., Nelson, E. E., Rusch, B. D., Fox, A. S., Oakes, T. R., & Davidson, R. J. (2004, February) Orbitofrontal cortex tracks positive mood in mothers viewing pictures of their newborn infants. *Neuroimage,* 21(2), 583-592.

Park, A. (2007, August 6). Baby Einsteins: Not so smart after all. *Time.*

Phillips-Silver, J., & Trainor, L. J. (2005, June). Feeling the beat: Movement influences infant rhythm perception. *Science,* 308(5727), 1430.

Websites

aplaceofourown.net/question_detail.php?id=355—information about infant brain development

babyzone.com/baby/a1849—enjoying your baby from day 1 to year 1

bananasinc.org/uploads/1126298158.pdf—developmental milestones for 0–12 months

brilliantbaby.com—activities to create a happier and smarter child

drgreene.com—answers to common pregnancy and parenting questions.

ed.gov/parents/earlychild/ready/healthystart/fourmonth.pdf—month by month developmental activities for babies 0–12 months

fisher-price.com—information on infant growth

littlekidsgamesonline.com/newborn-babies.html—games for newborns

nccic.org/pubs/goodstart/state-infant-elg.html—child care guidelines for all states

ncsmartstart.org/index.htm—The North Carolina partnership for children

parents.com/parents—lots of information about babies

pbs.org/parents/earlylearning/parentese.html—information about raising babies and preschoolers

preksmarties.com—articles about teaching babies, infant intelligence and infant stimulation

reading.org—International Reading Association

smartbaby.com

whitehouse.gov/firstlady/ed_8month_text.pdf—files similar to this also available for ages from birth to 12 months

zerotothree.org—everything you want to know about infants

PowerPoint Presentation

Word segmentation: Effects of the native language and of the native dialect by Thierry Nazzi, *Laboratoire Psychologie de la Perception, CNRS,* Université Paris.

INDEX